THE LIFE AND ART
OF CLAUDE MONET

THE LIFE AND ART OF CLAUDE MONET:

Impressions of France

JOHN RUSSELL TAYLOR

CRESCENT BOOKS
NEW YORK•AVENEL

First published in Great Britain in 1995
by Collins & Brown Limited
London House
Great Eastern Wharf
Parkgate Road
London SW11 4NQ

This 1995 edition published by Crescent Books, distributed byRandom House Value
Publishing, Inc., 40 Engelhard Avenue, Avenel, New Jersey 07001

Random House
New York•Toronto•London•Sydney•Auckland

FRONT COVER: *The Poppies at Argenteuil*, Claude Monet, 1873.

BACK COVER: Photograph of Claude Monet with his step-daughters at Giverny, *c*.1917.

FRONTISPIECE: *The Basin at Argenteuil*, Claude Monet, 1872.

HALF-TITLE: *View of Rouen*, Claude Monet, 1883 (black crayon on scratchboard).

A CIP Catalog record for this book is available from the Library of Congress.

ISBN 0517 12033 X

Conceived, designed and edited by Collins & Brown Limited

Senior Editor: Catherine Bradley
Editor: Elizabeth Drury
Picture Research and captions: Sara Waterson
Art Director: Roger Bristow
Senior Art Editor: Ruth Hope
Designer: Claire Graham
Design assistance from: Kevin Williams
Map: Eugene Fleury

Reproduction by Typongraph, Italy

Printed and bound in Hong Kong by Dai Nippon

CONTENTS

ℐNTRODUCTION

WHEN PAUL CÉZANNE WAS asked his opinion of his old friend and colleague, Claude Monet, his verdict was, 'Only an eye. But what an eye!' Such a view ignores the manifold evidence in Monet's work of careful planning and deep thought; but in one obvious respect Cézanne was right. Everything in Monet began with the act of seeing. And so what he saw - precisely what he saw - was uniquely important to his life and his art. The exact location always matters, and Monet's movements in search of inspiration for his landscapes become the best, indeed the only, way of relating his story.

The eye is not always passive, although at the beginning it probably was. Monet's childhood home was Le Havre. His first important influence, the man who actually persuaded him to try his hand at painting, was Eugène Boudin, the great master of the Channel coast beach scene. What could be more natural than that the teenage Monet's first essays in painting in oils should be of the sights with which he had grown up? When he went to Paris to study, he must have been tempted to paint the rapidly changing scenes in front of and all around him. The fashionable term for this, coined by Charles Baudelaire, was that they should be 'painters of modern life': such was the ideal for the young painters around Edouard Manet. This essentially meant being painters of Paris, the modern city *par excellence*.

This Monet was, or tried to be, on occasion. But already his pictures of fashionable life and

LEFT: **Self-Portrait of the Artist Wearing a Beret, 1886.** *By the time of this rare self-portrait, Monet had made his reputation by following his own path. This picture shows the confidence and determination of the artist at the height of his powers.*

sport tended to be located in leafy glades, which could have been anywhere, or in some of the more rustic-looking nooks and corners around Paris, such as the riverside bathing place La Grenouillère. He even raged to his friend and confidant Jean-Frédéric Bazille, with whom, when they were struggling young painters, he shared a studio, that he never felt right in town: for real inspiration he had to return to the 'reality' of nature and the countryside. From taking his world for granted, he was already learning to impose his own standards on it, to look positively for it, instead of accepting it unthinkingly because it happened to be there.

Some of Monet's early changes of scene were enforced. Without the intervention of the outer world of politics he would never have gone to London or Holland in 1870–1871. However, he had to go into exile, first to escape conscription in the Franco-Prussian War, and then to avoid the worse horrors of the Siege of Paris and the Commune. Yet the visual experiences

LEFT: **The Petite Creuse, 1888-89.** *One of a series of iridescent studies of the river valley, painted against the light. The 'terrible savagery' of the rocky landscapes was to fascinate and inspire Monet.*

so gained would all be valuable to him, and the time in London probably sowed the seed that was later to blossom in his unforgettable evocations of iridescent smog upon the Thames. When he and his new family returned to France, he chose to live near, but not in, Paris, downstream in the little town, not yet quite suburbanized, of Argenteuil.

This, to begin with, suited him very well as a painter. He could turn away from the belching factory chimneys and half-close his eyes so that the brash new housing merged comfortably into the landscape. But finally the changes in Argenteuil became too much for him. It was becoming too like the urban environment from which he thought he had escaped. He therefore moved progressively further away from the centre, first to Vétheuil and then to Giverny. Whatever the practical reasons of finance and family that necessitated these moves, more than anything else they were undertaken to appease, if not satisfy, the hunger of the eye.

Nothing could satisfy it totally. Throughout the 1880s he travelled endlessly, in relentless quest of the perfect scene, the ideal moment. He was in the grip of some kind of compulsion. It has been conjectured that part of the reason for his journeying at this time was that he was uncomfortable with his 'irregular' domestic arrangements. Discretion may well have had something to do with his long absences from home in Giverny, but it can have been only a small part. Always paramount was the need of the artist to find the right subject, to make a change when he needed change. He would wander irritably up and down the Channel coast, looking for this elusive rock formation or that expressive change in the weather that would 'speak' to him and compel him to paint it. No longer a slave to his surroundings, they were still of primary importance in his artistic inspiration.

Travel could still bring revelations. His first trip to Provence and the Mediterranean coast was an instance of this. He went down there initially

ABOVE: *A panoramic photograph of Rouen in the late nineteenth century. Monet had close family ties to the city, a busy industrial centre and port on the river Seine.*

as a tourist with Auguste Renoir, to see their old friend Cézanne in his family home at Aix. But Monet was so captivated by the unbelievable light and colour, the long, slowly changing southern days, which gave him time to capture fleeting effects in paint, that shortly afterwards he had to sneak back by himself (he could not work, he said, with others around him, even with such a good friend as Renoir) to work intensively and make the new landscape his own. Shortly after, another trip to an unfamiliar area had an even more radical effect. Taken to the valley of the Creuse, he was so enthralled by the way the harsh, brazen light beat down upon and rebounded off the bare, rocky landscape that he realized the only way he could do it justice was by painting in series: essentially the same scene from the same viewpoint at different times of day.

Possibly as a result of this experience, Monet began to realize that finally the only things worth painting were inside his own head. A trigger from objective experience might still be necessary, but once his imagination was fired he could supply the rest himself. He did not physically need to be in front of Rouen Cathedral or looking out at the Thames from the Savoy – or not for long. Whatever he noted down on the spot, he would develop and harmonize and refine later on, alone in his studio. And if he created the scene mentally, why should he not re-create it physically? In the last years at Giverny he painted what he saw, around his house or in his water-garden. By then he had finally achieved complete control over his physical environment. He had to see the water lily in order to be inspired to paint it. But then he himself had first put the water lily there, arranged its context, taking account of the exact direction from which the sun would strike it and how the shadow would fall from an overhanging tree. He was Giverny, but that was because, first of all, Giverny was a projection of himself.

ABOVE: *Monet in his final years, standing by the water-lily pond at Giverny. The wisteria-covered Japanese footbridge is in the background.*

LE HAVRE: THE EARLY YEARS

LEFT: **Farmyard in Normandy, c.1863.** *This early painting by Monet depicts a familiar childhood scene in the Normandy countryside, now under threat from creeping industrialization. Following Manet's example, the painting combines realism with a stylistic abstraction that draws the eye to each element of the painting in turn.*

OSCAR-CLAUDE MONET WAS born in Paris, in the rue Laffitte close to Montmartre, on 14 November 1840. His father was a grocer who in 1845 was doing so badly that he decided to sell up and go to Le Havre, where his half-sister lived. She was married to a wholesale grocer and ship's chandler, Jacques Lecadre, and Monet's father joined the business. The move was from a relatively affluent part of Paris (Napoleon III was born in the street where the Monets lived, and Lola Montes, the famous equestrienne mistress of Ludwig I of Bavaria, lived there), and Monet's mother seems to have taken the view that she had married beneath her, Adolphe Monet being her second and much less successful husband.

At the time the Monets arrived there, Le Havre was in a state of particular prosperity. Trade with the English across the Channel was good, and it had never been more active as a fishing port, especially for herring. The town had, as well as salt stores, factories for tobacco, sulphuric acid and starch. In spite of being one of the busiest and most commercial of the French ports, it continued to attract visitors. Situated on the northern coast of Normandy, just across the estuary of the Seine from the more evidently picturesque Honfleur and Trouville, it was a good centre from which to enjoy the coastal scenery. This was the background to Monet's childhood, and he was later to say, 'I have stayed faithful to the sea by which I grew up.'

BELOW: *A photograph probably taken in the 1870s shows the developing seafront at Le Havre, with its fine new buildings and crowded harbour. Monet, a frequent visitor to his family at nearby Sainte-Adresse, must have watched the growth of his home town with interest.*

Caricature in France

IN THE MID-NINETEENTH CENTURY names such as Daumier, Gavarni, Doré and Grandville were among the most famous in the French art world. Not, of course, the grandest, because they were for the most part merely caricaturists, but franc for franc they were probably as prosperous as any. Certainly knowledge of their work spread to classes of French society that had never heard of Ingres or Delacroix, Corot or Courbet.

The beginning of this golden age of French caricature was in 1839, when the series of designs, *Les Français peints par eux-mêmes*, began to appear. It was published by subscription, in 422 parts, and was the brainchild of the editor Léon Curmer. Slightly more remotely, it was the brainchild of the English writer and editor Kenny Meadows, who published in the same year a two-volume miscellany of literary and visual caricature portraits of English types, *Heads of the People*. This was rapidly translated into French for Curmer as a companion piece to his own publication. Both of these works, and the imitations on the subject of the Spanish, the Germans, the Dutch and the Russians that immediately followed in France, were strongly influenced by the current vogue for the science of phrenology. This claimed to be able to classify humanity according to the shape of a person's skull, which could enable the individual's dominant traits to be 'read'. There was a related artistic craze for identifying parallels between man and the animal kingdom and basing visual characterizations on the fancied similarity between, say, an elderly suitor and an old goat.

This kind of caricature was more or less the only option after the imposition of strict laws censoring political satire by the Orléans monarchy in 1835. Artists in this line became depictors of manners in general terms rather than satirists of particular political movements or figures. This was the form that those such as Daumier, Gavarni, Grandville and others carried to new heights, both of accomplishment and popularity.

Caricature of this largely non-political type was the rage throughout the Second Empire. (Freedom of the press, having been revived under the Second Republic, was promptly withdrawn when Louis Napoleon became emperor.) Even in a provincial town like Le Havre, it would have been difficult for an intelligent boy such as Monet not to be aware of this kind of art: the illustrated papers were immensely popular and within reach of everybody. Curiously, the teenage Monet's work most closely resembles that of an exact contemporary, Louis-Alexandre Gossit de Guines, who published under the name of André Gill. It is intriguing to speculate on the direction Monet might have taken if, instead of being taken under the wing of Boudin, he had been, like the teenage Gill, taken up by the photographer and satirist Nadar (Félix Tournachon). Significantly, however, the paths of Nadar and Monet were to cross in Paris. Monet and others of the Impressionist group were interested in the aerial perspective of Nadar's photographs.

Some examples of caricatures by the young Monet, showing distinctive animal characteristics.
LEFT: *People of the Theatre*; RIGHT: *A Man with a Large Nose.*

When he was ten, Monet went to the local school in the rue de la Mailleraye, where he was distinguished mainly for his ungovernable behaviour and erratic attendance. During lessons, he later claimed, he did very little except decorate the margins of his school books with scribbles and sketches. However, all the evidence of his maturity suggests that one way or another he was well educated. He was able to keep pace with the intellectuals with whom he later associated, and he possessed, when he chose to display it, an excellent prose style and a gift for verbal self-expression relatively rare in painters of his circle.

Monet seems not to have got on at all well with his school's drawing-master, François-Charles Ochard, a pupil of Jacques-Louis David. He was clearly gifted, but inclined to be perverse and impudent. His cheek began to pay off quite early. The studies he made in class soon took the form of caricatures, in profile or full face, of his fellow pupils and his teachers. These were received with such enthusiasm – though not necessarily by the victims – that his fame as a caricaturist spread, and when he was 15 he was asked by a local picture-framer and seller of paintings to exhibit some of his work in the shop window. People even proved willing to pay for his caricatures and commissioned him to make more. By the time he left school he already had it in mind to become a professional artist as an alternative to going into the family business.

There were at that time a number of successful caricaturists and artists of the grotesque, Henri Daumier among them. Daumier was 32 years older than Monet and then at the height of his fame as a satirical draughtsman. The young Monet must have known of Daumier's work as it appeared in various popular magazines: his surviving caricatures, signed '0. Monet', have a resemblance to Daumier's work that can hardly be accidental. They also bear witness to an extraordinary technical facility for one who was, in effect, self-taught.

Monet might have made his living as a cartoonist had it not been for one very important encounter. This was with Eugène Boudin, the most prominent of the local painters. Le Havre did not have much artistic life of its own, but

RIGHT: *François-Charles Ochard (Monet's teacher). Monet remarked that 'School seemed to me like a prison' and that his schoolbooks were filled with 'ultra-fantastic ornaments, and the faces and profiles of my teachers shown in the most irreverent light'. In the later 1850s he sold these more finished caricatures to family friends and to the notables of Le Havre.*

it was frequented by painters from Paris. Boudin was the exception. After training in Paris and trying to make a career for himself there, he had returned to Normandy in 1853-4 and would continue to live on the Normandy coast, with a few interruptions, for the rest of his life. He was not treated with particular regard by the locals because his practice of painting sea and beach scenes in the open air was considered eccentric, and he did not seem to make much money by it. To begin with, Monet shared the conventional doubts, but eventually it was through Boudin that a turning-point was reached. As he wrote in 1920 to Gustave Geffroy (who was later to publish a biography of Monet in 1922):

Yes, I did meet Boudin in Le Havre. He was, I think, fifteen years older than me, and I was at that time trying my hardest to make a name for myself as a caricaturist. I was about fifteen, and I had become known throughout Le Havre: I charged 15 to 20 francs for a portrait and signed them 'Oscar', my second name. [It was actually his first.] I often showed them in close proximity to Boudin's, but to begin with I did not like his painting at all, being then under the influence of academic ideas on art. One day Boudin said to me: 'You've got talent. You should give up this sort of work; you'll get fed up with it anyway, sooner or later. Your sketches are excellent, but you shouldn't stop there. Do as I do: learn to draw properly and value the sea, the light, the blue sky.' I took his advice, and we used to go on long expeditions together, when I could paint things directly from nature. That way, I came to understand nature and love it passionately. I also became more and more appreciative of Boudin's light-filled paintings. I can only repeat that I owe all I have done to Boudin, and all the success I have achieved.

Monet's response to the lesson of Boudin was, as Geffroy was to comment, in the nature of a religious conversion. Boudin's financial circumstances

Le Havre

L E HAVRE IN 1845 must have seemed quite a comedown for the five-year-old Monet's parents after Paris. Although it was at the seaward end of the Seine, reasonably accessible by steamboat and railway, it appeared to be the essence of provinciality. But contemporary sources tell a different story. Who would imagine, for instance, that you could at that time take ship directly from Le Havre to Rotterdam or Hamburg, and even to St Petersburg via Copenhagen? There exists an illuminating piece of evidence on the state of Le Havre in the 1840s in the shape of *Itinéraire des bateaux à vapeur de Paris au Havre*, a popular publication that reached its fifth revised edition before the fall of King Louis-Philippe in 1848.

The description of Le Havre that it contains begins with some elaborate verses by a local poetaster, who signed himself Cas. Delavigne:

...Charming town!
It was my cradle: gentle climate, fertile soil,
Friendly people, a site as pretty as a picture.
After Constantinople there is nowhere so beautiful.

The text notes that the population is 23,816, that it is the seat of the sub-prefecture, stock exchange, courts and chamber of commerce, and that, though not an ancient town, it has been making very rapid advances in importance owing to its splendid port facilities and thriving local industries.

Le Havre was, to begin with, a fishing port. Positioned at the mouth of the Seine, it was the most accessible and capacious port on the coast, capable of holding many very large merchant vessels in its

BELOW: *A print of Le Havre made in about 1845, the year of Monet's birth. The bustle of these quays must have been a familiar sight to the artist throughout his youth.*

outer port and three large inner basins, while even larger ships could ride at anchor in the roads, no further away, as the *Itinéraire* points out, than a cannon shot from land. Though the military allusion was to prove irrelevant, its significance was not entirely metaphorical: in the early 1850s, when the establishment of the Second Empire raised a few imperial bogies in the minds of the British across the Channel, Le Havre was ready to assume a military character if required.

Set on the edge of a fertile plain scattered with woods, parks and châteaux, the town itself had rapidly developed from being (according to the *Itinéraire*) 'mournful, dirty and unhealthy', into a veritable second metropolis: 'the main street, the rue de Paris, is truly worthy of the capital itself: straight, very wide, a paved highway decorated with sidewalks and edged with beautiful houses...it presents at all hours the most animated spectacle.' The account seems to be designed rather to impress the visiting businessman than to encourage searchers

after the picturesque. But while the town was said to offer relatively little of historical or anecdotal interest, the countryside around was fulsomely praised, and the view of Le Havre from nearby Ingouville was said to be 'ravishing'. It was, therefore, hardly surprising that as soon as artists turned to landscape, as they did increasingly in the 1840s, Le Havre and the surrounding Normandy coast should become a magnet for them. Another attraction was the presence of Eugène Boudin, born in Honfleur in 1826, who was regarded as so promising a painter that in 1851 the Le Havre authorities gave him a grant to study in Paris. He returned to Normandy in 1854 and met the teenage Monet in 1856.

BELOW: *A photograph of the Le Havre seafront in the 1870s. The growing prosperity of the town is reflected in the fine buildings and numerous ships.*

could hardly have inspired a desire to emulate him: when Monet first knew him, he could scarcely keep the wolf from the door and painted any number of small pictures that he sold, if he was lucky, by the dozen for derisory sums. But Boudin encouraged in him the passion for painting. In 1858 Monet executed his first painting in oils, the little *View at Rouelles*, and under Boudin's auspices it was hung that year in the annual municipal exhibition.

Monet's mother had died early in 1857 and from that time he tended to be on bad terms with his father. The obvious step was to follow Boudin's advice: in addition to developing the technique of painting directly from nature, he needed some serious academic training, and Paris was undoubtedly the place for this. He applied twice to the municipality of Le Havre for a grant for these studies, and was twice refused. The grounds of the second refusal have been preserved in the municipal archives under the date 16 May 1859. The wording suggests that Monet's caricatures had been a little too near the knuckle:

Monet, Oscar, having worked with Messieurs Ochard, Wissant and Boudin, presents with his application a still-life by which we might judge his talent, if it were not so completely demonstrated by those lively sketches of his that we all know. Along the way his remarkable natural gifts have taken him up to now – in caricature, to call a spade a spade – Oscar Monet has already found popularity, so slow to come to serious works. But is there not a danger in this precocious success, in the direction his facile pencil has taken till now: that of keeping the young artist away from more serious but less agreeable studies? These alone have the right to municipal liberality. Time alone will tell.

Although he was denied municipal support, Monet was not completely without means. His father was not in a position to assist him much financially, but his aunt, Marie-Jeanne Lecadre, childless and an amateur painter

ABOVE: **A Street in Normandy, 1864**. *One of a pair of canvases showing the rue de la Bavolle, Honfleur, in the early afternoon. Monet carefully noted the variations in the scene a few moments can produce by distinctions of colour and elongation of their shadows.*

RIGHT: **The Pointe de la Hève at Low Tide, 1865.** *One of two large canvases submitted by Monet and accepted by the Salon of 1865, becoming his first works shown in Paris. Their size was a bold bid for attention amid the crowded offerings, whilst the subject allied him to well-known* plein-air *landscapists, such as Jongkind and Boudin, who were active around Honfleur in the 1860s.*

herself, seems to have taken the place of his mother and had set aside for him a little fund of 2,000 francs. (At that time it was possible to live decently, if modestly, in Paris on about 120 francs a month.) He determined to submit the two still-lifes he had brought with him to Paris to Constant Troyon, a successful landscape painter, noted for his pictures of cattle, whom he may have met in Le Havre. It was perhaps Gravier who wrote the letter of introduction to Troyon to which Monet referred in his first letter to Boudin from Paris. (It is dated 19 May 1859, so clearly Monet did not wait for the outcome of his second application to the Le Havre council before leaving for Paris.) Monet quoted in some detail Troyon's advice to him, after passing on Troyon's warmest regards to Boudin and the offer that, if Boudin were to send a batch of seascapes, landscapes and still-lifes, Troyon would undertake to sell them, provided that 'they are more finished than those you have sent him before'.

BELOW: *Honfleur, an ancient port on the mouth of the Seine estuary opposite Le Havre, was already much visited in the late 1870s. This postcard shows the marketplace and the picturesque old church of St Catherine soon after it was painted by Monet.*

I showed him my two still-lifes. His comment was: 'My dear fellow, your colour is fine: the effect really works. But you really must apply yourself to some serious study. All this is excellent as far as it goes, but it comes very easily to you: it's something you will always have, come what may. If you take my advice and are serious about art, you will start by enrolling in a studio that concentrates on figure painting. Learn to draw: that is where most of you youngsters fall short today. Pay attention and you'll see that I'm right. Draw for all you are worth; you can never learn too much. But don't neglect painting. Go into the country every so often to sketch, and whatever you do be sure to work the sketches through. Copy pictures at the Louvre. Don't be a stranger: come and see me and show me what you're doing. With courage you'll get there.'

Armed with these words of encouragement from a successful artist (unlike Boudin at this period), Monet overcame his family's objections to his taking up painting. They agreed to let him stay on for a month or two and really work at his drawing. Then he might return to Le Havre for the summer, make some of those sketches and studies recommended by Troyon and return to Paris for serious study in the winter.

During this first brief period in Paris, Monet met Amand Gautier through an introduction from his aunt. Gautier was a much less conventional artist than Troyon, being a follower of Gustave Courbet, the celebrated painter of landscapes (see page 29). Gautier was an *habitué* of the Brasserie des Martyrs, haunt of the Realist painters, and it was no doubt through him that Monet met, then or later, such important figures as Alphonse Legros, Henri Fantin-Latour and Carolus-Duran, who was to paint a portrait of the young Monet. Though he did not, for all his self-confidence, recognize it at the time, the course that his life was to take was already determined. Time, as the Le Havre council concluded, would tell.

PARIS: THE BOHEMIAN YEARS

ABOVE: *A xylograph caricature by Grandville, 1844, lampooning the slavish copying, often from plaster casts, which formed the basis of academic art-school teaching of the period.*

LEFT: **The Beach at Sainte-Adresse, 1867.** *Monet frequently painted this beach, exploring the relationship between the sky and sea, and the effect of the changing weather.*

DURING THE SUMMER OF 1859, which he spent in Le Havre, Monet seems to have met Johan Barthold Jongkind, a painter of seascapes much admired by Troyon. In the autumn he returned to Paris. There was some question as to where he should go for the academic training that it was generally agreed he needed. Troyon had suggested the studio of Thomas Couture, one of the most successful painters and teachers of the time, but Monet disregarded this advice since he did not at all approve of Couture's own painting. Instead, he chose to go to a free studio, the Académie Suisse, where poor painters could work from live models at little cost. Here, almost certainly, he met the first of those who were to be an important influence on him in Paris: the 29-year old Camille Pissarro, who was among a 'little band of landscape painters' at that time wrestling with human anatomy at the Académie Suisse.

The art life of Paris was still at that period dominated by the official Salon (see pages 60–61), a self-perpetuating repository of the academic tradition that was regarded, by even the most wayward, as the road to success. The great argument, which continued to rumble on, was between the followers of Jean Auguste Dominique Ingres, with his devotion to clear outlines and accurate draughtsmanship, and Eugène Delacroix, with his dramatic use of colour and cultivation of the visible brushstroke. (Ingres believed, by contrast, that all evidence of human handiwork in a painting should be rigorously suppressed.) Delacroix was constantly rejected by the Salon though he continued to submit paintings. He was not the only great non-conformist, however. More recently the star of Courbet had risen, representing another challenge to academic conformity: he stood for ruthless realism, painting things as they really were (or at any rate as he perceived them) rather than

ABOVE: *A photograph of Monet aged about 20. His taste for the fine things of life developed early; Monet patronized the best tailor in Paris, and Renoir remembered his friend as a great dandy: 'He was penniless yet he wore lace at his wrists!'*

subordinating them to all kinds of academic rules about suitable subjects and how far an idealizing veil should be cast over the sometimes ugly truth.

Matters had come to a minor crisis in 1855, when Courbet had two important pictures rejected out-of-hand from the official French pavilion at the Exposition Universelle of that year and defiantly showed them in a pavilion of his own just outside. Those officially in charge were not to be swayed by such happenings and continued to reject anything that did not meet their rigid standards. In 1859 resistance moved a stage further: the Salon rejected works by Edouard Manet, an elegant young man-about-town who had aimed firmly at conventional success by training with Couture; Fantin-Latour, known principally as a flower-painter; and an eccentric young American called James McNeill Whistler, who was very talented, combative and spoiling for a fight. The rejected paintings from the Salon were hung in a private studio, and they created something of a stir in official artistic circles. It was beginning to be recognized that the future of art in Paris might, perhaps, lie outside the academies after all.

Monet's ideas on all this were probably not precisely formulated at this time, and certainly he does not seem to have set out with any radically new ideas. Among the artists later to be known as the Impressionists, he was by no means unique in this. Manet, the most senior, never veered from his belief that success, if it was to be achieved, must come from fighting his way into the Salon rather than sitting outside gnashing his teeth. (In fact, he was never to show in any of the Impressionists' independent exhibitions that were later to become so important.) Two of the others in Paris in the late 1850s, Pissarro and Edgar Degas, were not adopting revolutionary stances either. But Monet was by nature rather awkward, confident, even bumptious, and not necessarily ready to do things the way others said they had to be done unless he himself saw good reason for it. His connections through Gautier with the Realists of the Brasserie des Martyrs were hardly

ABOVE: *The Pont-Neuf in Paris linked the traditional bohemian artists' quarter of the Left Bank with the central area near to the Louvre and the rue de Rivoli. The quay of the Ile de la Cité, over which the bridge passes, can be seen on the right of the photograph.*

conducive to toeing the academic line; nor were the anarchist political ideas of Pissarro, developed in the five years he had been in Paris and ever more clearly defined once he had finished with his formal training at the Ecole des Beaux-Arts.

Before Monet had the opportunity to settle down, his career was interrupted by conscription into the army, which was determined by a type of lottery. He was called up for a seven-year stretch and despatched to Algeria. In later life he told Geffroy that he was enchanted by the place and by the whole experience. While serving with the Chasseurs d'Afrique in Oran he met the young Pierre-Benoît Delpech from Normandy, who became a lifelong friend. Sixty years later they still saw each other regularly, and in 1919 Delpech brought to show him a batch of drawings and watercolours done by Monet during his military service that Delpech had kept. Enchanted or not by Algeria, Monet does not appear to have resisted when, after some 18 months, his aunt managed to buy him out of the army.

The Paris to which Monet returned in the autumn of 1862 was already rather different from the city he had left. For one thing, resistance to the Salon was beginning to harden. In 1860 the Salon had once again rejected several significant works, and this time there was a really large-scale rival show by those who had been refused, including Delacroix, Courbet, Jean Baptiste Camille Corot and Jean François Millet, along with painters of the so-called Barbizon school, who made it a principle to paint in the open air (*en plein air*). Meanwhile, the streets and buildings of Paris were changing apace. By 1860 Napoleon III's plans to turn Paris into a new, modern metropolis, elaborated by Baron Haussmann, were being enthusiastically carried out.

Twelve years before, when the monarchy of Louis-Philippe was finally swept away, to be replaced by the short-lived Second Republic and then by the Empire of Napoleon III, Paris was still essentially a medieval city. Its centre at this time consisted of a rabbit warren of winding lanes and alleys bearing heavily on the river that ran through it. Neither Napoleon III nor

ABOVE: *A view of the rue Zacharie, showing the typically narrow alleyways and vibrant street-life threatened by Haussmann's dramatic plans for modernization.*

his lieutenant, Haussmann, had any patience with that. Clearly, to be the capital of a modern state and a focus of international attention, Paris had to be dragged out of the Dark Ages. Haussmann's solution was to flatten much of the old centre, driving wide boulevards and avenues through the rookeries and clearing buildings away from the banks of the Seine to make great heroic vistas. In the process the old social pattern of the *quartiers* that had existed for centuries was irrevocably disrupted.

The city that Monet and his new friends chose to live in during the 1860s was the quintessence of urbanization, a hub of activity and excitement for those with a taste for change. For aspiring artists, all the official exhibitions that counted, all the most influential teachers, all the best schools, beckoned them to Paris.

It is difficult to discern Monet's feelings about Paris from his work. When he first arrived there he concentrated on still-life painting, a subject not so much fashionable as convenient, since he did not have to hire models or leave his studio. (Monet's friend Frédéric Bazille, writing to his family in 1866, begged them for some money so that he would be able to afford a model and not be condemned to 'perpetual still-lifes'.) While he was living in Paris in the 1860s, however, Monet seems to have painted a wide variety of subjects, including landscapes. Not all of these were views of Paris. In the spring of 1860 he went on a painting expedition to Champigny-sur-Marne with a group of friends that almost certainly included Pissarro; he

Nineteenth-Century French Landscape

UNDER THE FIRST REPUBLIC and the Empire public commissions bulked large in the artistic world, and these, naturally, were for historical, allegorical and religious subjects. In the realm of easel painting historical subjects were most in demand, and of course there was always a market for portraits. Landscape was less recognized but still had its place; either in the form of 'historical landscape' (essentially landscape disguised as history painting by the insertion of a small mythological or historical subject); or of rural landscape (a country scene, usually tame and cultivated, in which no human figures were necessary at all, although a few incidentals were normally present).

In 1800 a book entitled *Eléments de perspective pratique*, by the painter Pierre-Henri de Valenciennes, was published as a guide to would-be painters. It recommended them to seek subjects in their own native environment and sketch them on the spot, for working-up later in the studio into paintings for exhibition. Thus the Romantic response to nature was recognized as a suitable subject for art, provided it were filtered and domesticated. In 1817 an official Prix de Rome, eagerly competed for by young painters, added landscape to the classes of competition for the first time, and in 1818 the painter Jean Baptiste Depertes published his *Théorie de paysage*, which elaborated and systematized Valenciennes's ideas on landscape. This contained a curiously egalitarian note of approval for landscape as being easier for the uneducated to respond to than, for example, history painting, since no specialist preliminary knowledge was required to interpret it.

This was clearly a straw in the wind, indicative of the continuing rise of the relatively untutored bourgeoisie as a potential market for art. Depertes emphasized Valenciennes's view that on-the-spot observation was necessary for good landscape painting and reiterated the classical view that, while a high degree of finish was necessary for the history painting, a rustic landscape could legitimately be left much rougher. As the century advanced, these notions helped to create a climate of opinion very favourable to the landscape. While centre-stage was

The two giants of the plein-air *school of landscape painting. As painters of the natural world, both Corot's delicacy of touch and Courbet's more robust realism strongly influenced the Impressionist group.* LEFT: *Corot at Arras in 1871;* RIGHT: *Courbet at about the same date.*

held by Ingres and Delacroix (to neither of whom was landscape of particular interest), landscape was quietly taking an ever-larger proportion of the market. By mid-century it was even challenging history painting as the genre most patronized by the State.

During the 1840s and 1850s the Salon was plentifully hung with landscapes, and though painters such as Courbet, Millet and Corot still had trouble with the Académie and the Salon, they were nevertheless financially among the most successful painters of their day. All of them were exponents of rustic landscape: centrally in Corot's case, very importantly in Millet's and prominently even in Courbet's, this being one of the less shocking forms in which the rebel Realist could express his view of life. In addition, the Barbizon school of painters, a group of Parisians who took to the woods south of Paris in the 1840s in search of back-to-nature inspiration, was already trading successfully on the growing taste of an uneducated, non-specialist public for landscape. When the Impressionists started painting landscapes in the 1860s, it was by no means a fantastic notion that it might be the fastest route to fame and fortune.

Not all the Impressionists were specially dedicated to landscape painting in the 1860s, or indeed at any stage in their lives. Manet and Degas, the two who most clearly set out to be 'painters of modern life', seldom painted a pure landscape throughout their respective careers. Whatever their earliest ambitions, however, most of the Impressionists were seen by contemporaries as predominately landscape painters and this was by and large how they aimed at Salon success. The main problem the Impressionists encountered in official circles was the perceived lack of 'finish' in their work. Monet, for one, was very aware of the criticism, and carefully distinguished between paintings that he produced with a Salon showing in mind, and those that he created for his own satisfaction, As late as January 1880 he was still wondering if he might not acheive a breakthrough at the Salon, and with this in mind painted three large wintry scenes on the frozen Seine. (They had to be large because the Salon required it if one wanted to make a major impact there.) In the event, Monet submitted two of the three, of which one was accepted, but held back the third as being 'too much to my own taste to submit'. Clearly it was acceptable in the Salon to have made studies for a big formal landscape on the spot. What was less acceptable to the Salon authorities, however, constituted the essence of landscape for Monet: that it should look as if it were painted completely on the spot, offering a fleeting impression of a single moment.

BELOW: *A cartoon by Daumier from the popular satirical magazine Le Charivari of May 1865. It was captioned 'The Landscapists: the First copies from Nature – the Second copies from the First'.*

also went on longer trips, home to Le Havre and to the Normandy coast. This was precisely what Troyon had advised Monet to do on his first trip to Paris (see page 21). Such expeditions had by now become part of the academic painter's routine, if he painted landscapes at all – and more and more of the academic painters did, as by the end of the 1840s it had become clear that landscapes ideally suited the new class of art buyers. These were members of the prosperous urban bourgeoisie, who liked to feel that the country was there, safe and unchanging, even if they were seldom inclined to suffer its less comfortable aspects themselves. Consequently, the painter assumed the role of surrogate traveller, presenting the evidence of his travels for the vicarious pleasure of town-dwellers. While sketching from nature had been advocated by the academies since at least 1800, the corollary was always that the painting itself should be done in the studio, and should in various ways impose order and ideal form upon the raw material first noted. The idea of showing an 'impression' for its own sake (see page 64) was unthinkable.

It was natural that Monet, with his upbringing beside the sea, should be more sympathetic to the world outside Paris than some of his fellows. With his paintings of Le Havre and its surroundings, he was the first and principal artist of his generation to paint seascapes. The slightly older Boudin was working mainly on beach scenes at this time, but these were crowded with figures, and the sea played only a subordinate part. Yet Monet seems also to have enjoyed the metropolitan release of bohemian life, and spent time with others from the future Impressionist group sitting in artists' cafés talking passionately on the issues of the day. At about this time he allegedly, like his friend Pissarro, held strongly left-wing views, but he readily painted portraits, figure scenes and occasional townscapes recording the new, grander Paris that was emerging as a result of Haussmann's efforts.

ABOVE: *A watercolour sketch of painters at the Ferme St Siméon by Eugène Boudin in 1863. It shows, from left to right, Jongkind, Van Marche, Monet and 'Old Achard'. Bazille was also a frequent visitor to the Honfleur farm.*

RIGHT: **The Quai du Louvre**, 1867. *One of a group of oils painted in the mid 1860s that record the rapidly changing face of Paris. Monet obtained permission to work in the upper galleries of the Louvre; his viewpoint from above reflects that of the new topographical photographs widely published in France at the time.*

Haussmann and the New Paris

I N THE EARLY 1860S, when most of the painters later to be known as Impressionists first arrived in Paris, the city was in turmoil. Right in the middle of Napoleon III's reign, it was fairly stable politically, but physically the city was being totally transformed. On 18 November 1860 the Goncourt brothers wrote in their journal:

> Our Paris, the Paris where we were born, the Paris of the way of life of 1830 to 1848, is passing away. Its passing is not material but moral. Social life is going through a great evolution, which is beginning. I see women, children, households, families in this café. The interior is passing away. Life turns back to become public. The club for those on high, the café for those below, that is what society and the people are come to. All of this makes me feel, in this country so dear to my heart, like a traveller. I am a stranger to what is coming, to what is, as I am to these new boulevards, which no longer smack of the world of Balzac, which smack of London, some Babylon of the future. It is idiotic to arrive in an age under construction: the soul has discomforts as a result, like a man who lives in a newly built house.

The observation was not new. Writers had been complaining about the reckless modernization of Paris, the substitution of grandiose, faceless sameness for the old diversity and character, ever since 1830, when Victor Hugo had violently attacked Paris as it was and as it was becoming in a famous denunciatory description in *Notre Dame de Paris*. By the time of the Goncourts it was fashionable to blame one man, the Baron Georges-Eugène Haussmann, Prefect of the Seine under Napoleon III.

Haussmann, in his plans for the modernization of Paris, was simply following and systematizing tendencies that had already made themselves felt. The psychological and social centre of the city had been moving westward as grand new houses and public buildings were built outside the old city walls. Industry, as it developed from old-fashioned family trades, tended to seek more space on the periphery than it could ever hope to find in the centre.

To some extent it suited Haussmann's enemies to make out that he was much more efficient than in fact he ever managed to be in converting vision into bricks and stone. He conceived the city, for whatever combination of practical and theoretical reasons, according to Classical standards of regularity and symmetry. He envisaged such straight lines and striking prospects as anything in the palace and grounds of Versailles. To bring this about he had to move the workers out of the centre and flatten their slum dwellings. But he

LEFT: *Night-time work on the construction of arcades of the rue de Rivoli in 1854, using the novel illumination of electric light. In the foreground, work continues on the Hôtel du Louvre.*

also – much more embarrassingly – had to demolish new and imposing houses built by the rich and powerful to the west of the old city. Naturally there was opposition, not only from the artists who bewailed the loss of picturesqueness, but also from vested interests, sometimes with a voice at court or in the government.

All the same, Haussmann himself caught the imagination of the public, and so 'Haussmannization' became the label for all that he did and much that he did not do. And even so, there was no doubting the range and importance of the changes he did institute. It is estimated that by 1870 about one-fifth of all the streets in Paris were created by him, and when the works were at their most intense about a fifth of the total available workforce in Paris was employed in the building trades. After the fall of his master, Napoleon III, Haussmann lived quietly in retirement until his death in 1891, sometimes consulted, frequently argued over, as the modernization he had planned continued, very much as he had planned it, right through the Third Republic up to the end of the century. Gradually his worst enemies among the artists came to like the results of his work. Those who left the city, among them Monet and Renoir, probably did so in part because they were never reconciled to the new Paris.

However, Monet had never felt completely at home in the city, and by the end of his life he seems to have accepted Haussmann's Paris as completely as any of his fellows.

BELOW: *The completed buildings in 1855, showing the wide boulevards and Classical designs that were to dominate the new Paris.*

In the early years of the decade, just back from military service and with lost time to make up, Monet was eager to experience the life of the city. His father had been persuaded to help finance his studies in Paris on condition that he studied with the painter Charles Gleyre. Recommendation of Gleyre came once again through Monet's aunt. Her great-niece was married to a painter called Auguste Toulmouche, who was achieving some success at the Salon. Toulmouche had studied with Gleyre and proposed that Monet did likewise.

Monet entered Gleyre's *atelier* (studio) at the end of 1862, at the same time as Frédéric Bazille, who was from a prosperous family in Montpellier. They rapidly became close friends and met two other pupils at the *atelier*, Auguste Renoir and Alfred Sisley. Although an academic painter, Gleyre had a reputation for running his studio on very liberal lines. Later in life Monet gave a colourful account of his reception at Gleyre's:

> While we were drawing from a superb model, Gleyre came and criticized my work. 'It's not bad,' he said, 'but the breast is heavy, the shoulder too powerful, and the foot out of proportion.' 'I can only draw what I see,' I answered timidly. 'Praxiteles took the best elements from a hundred imperfect models to create a masterpiece,' Gleyre answered dryly. 'When you're doing something, you must always think of the antique.' That same evening I took Sisley, Renoir and Bazille aside. 'Let's get out of here,' I said. 'The place is unhealthy. They're lacking in sincerity.'

Despite these deficiencies, Monet continued to attend Gleyre's *atelier* on and off over a period of several years.

In 1863 epoch-making things were happening in the Paris art world. In particular there was the Salon des Refusés in which Manet's *Déjeuner sur l'herbe* caused a furore. The exhibition came about because the selection committee for the Salon rejected so many pictures that a direct appeal was made to the Emperor. He decreed that an alternative salon be set up, to open two weeks after the official Salon, in which the rejected artists could,

ABOVE: *A photograph of the carters' road through the Forest of Fontainebleau known as the Pavé de Chailly, taken in 1866. Monet made many visits to this area, often in company with other artists.*

BELOW: *The Ferme St Siméon near Honfleur, home for weeks on end to groups of artists, many from Paris. Meals would be taken communally in the garden, with a fertile exchange of ideas over flagons of wine or beer.*

RIGHT: **The Road from Chailly to Fontainebleau, 1864.** *An excellent example of Monet's frequent use of a wide-open foreground in his early work. This drew the spectator's eye into the painting and was possibly inspired by the enlargement of the foreground in landscape photography.*

if they wished, show their work. The result was a very heterogeneous collection of works, by no means all of which were in any way forward-looking or highly regarded. Manet's *Déjeuner* caused a sensation more on moral than aesthetic grounds (though it might be argued that here the two were not clearly distinguished). The Emperor thought it 'immodest' that a painter, even though relying on classical precedent for his composition, should combine female nudes (acceptable in a mythological context) with male figures in recognizably modern dress, in an umistakably real situation (presumably a woodland picnic of artists and models).

In all likelihood Monet was not in Paris to see the exhibition. In April and May he went with Bazille to the village of Chailly-en-Bière to paint. It was the first of many visits to the Forest of Fontainebleau. During the summer he was as usual in Le Havre, painting scenes in the Normandy countryside and on the coast. He was still going to Gleyre's during the winter of 1863-4, and quite possibly almost until it closed in July 1864.

Despite the excitement engendered by the official Salon des Refusés, acceptance by the official Salon remained the major goal of all the struggling artists in Paris. Everybody visited the Salon, everybody talked about it. The selection committee seems to have taken some account of the Salon des Refusés, and in 1865 Manet was accepted with, in some respects, an even more daring picture than the *Déjeuner*: his modern nude *Olympia*, which no-one was in much doubt represented a contemporary courtesan displaying herself before an unseen guest (the spectator, in effect). Also accepted, significantly, were a long list of names then unfamiliar to the general public, including Degas, Pissarro, Renoir and Berthe Morisot.Even Moner went some way towards justifying his family's sometimes shaky faith in him. by showing in the Salon two pictures, both painted at home on the Normandy coast, *Pointe de la Hève at Low Tide* (see page 19) and *The Seine Estuary at Honfleur* (see page 27). Nor did they go unrecognized; he was actually singled out for special praise by Paul Mantz in the *Gazette des Beaux-Arts* and by a critic signing himself Pigalle in the *Autographe*, who said of the second picture, 'M. Monet, unknown yesterday, has made a reputation with this single work.'

ABOVE: *A lithograph portrait of Berthe Morisot in 1872 by Manet, her close friend and future brother-in-law. Morisot was the first woman to be accepted as a full member of the Impressionist group, an unusual honour for the time. Monet respected her abilities greatly.*

Bazille: Colleague, Friend, Patron

AMONG MONET'S CONTEMPORARIES and friends, Jean-Frédéric Bazille was in some ways the most fortunate and in one obvious way the most unfortunate. His misfortune was his early death; he was killed, aged 29, by a stray bullet in the Franco-Prussian War. His fortune came from his family, prosperous old bourgeois from the south of France. Although letters show that he sometimes had to argue passionately with his father over his need for more money while studying in Paris, it seems that the money was always finally forthcoming. His origins were not as grand as those of Degas, nor as prosperous as those of Manet, but among his contemporaries in the group that gathered in the Café Guerbois he was certainly exceptional for his comparative affluence.

Spectacularly tall and thin, and from all accounts not at all interested in models and other such obliging ladies, Bazille stood apart from the group in a variety of other ways too. His closest friends were Renoir, Sisley and Monet, and although he never entirely followed them in their *plein-air* painting, or in the subordination of form to light, he was always more than generous to his impecunious friends with his time and money.

He also acted in some ways as a patron. Genuinely admiring of work very different from his own, he acquired a number of important early works by Monet and Renoir in particular. He even went beyond what he could easily afford in securing a small but helpful pension for Monet at one of his most difficult times. He also seems to have been extremely patient and long-suffering. At various stages he shared his studio with Renoir and with Monet, although after he and Monet had been turned out of the studio they shared in the rue Furstenberg (neighbours objected to the noise of a masked ball they organized there), Bazille confided to his brother, 'I must admit that I am not sorry to be living alone for a bit; sharing has many inconveniences, even when the two of you get on very well.'

Of his circle of friends, his main devotion seems to have been to Monet. When Monet was hard up (which was most of the time), he did all he could to find purchasers for his paintings, and even, at a time of some financial embarrassment for himself, bought Monet's *Women in the Garden* for the then considerable sum of 2,500 francs, which he had to pay in monthly instalments of 50 francs. He was constantly bombarded in the next months with begging letters from the penniless Monet.

Bazille possessed considerable organizing ability. He it was who first had the idea of organizing a Salon des Indépendants after the very poor showing he and his friends made in the selection for the 1867 Salon. His plan was for a group of young and not-so-young 'outsider' artists to hire a large studio and show there, free of the constraints of official academic attitudes. Although many of the artists he knew were willing to contribute, the final stumbling block was naturally, financial: the most their joint efforts could raise at this point was 2,500 francs, which was not enough to sustain the project. In this idea of Bazille's, however, lay the seeds that were eventually to germinate after his death with the holding of the first Impressionist exhibition of 1874.

RIGHT: *A photograph of the debonair Bazille, Monet's friend and champion, taken in 1869 shortly before his depature for war and premature death. His financial support was indispensible to Monet during the early years of struggle and poverty.*

Some such reassurance was sorely needed. In 1864 Monet was constantly at loggerheads with his family, chronically short of money and apparently able to rely only on Bazille for help and support. They had spent two months at Honfleur the previous summer, discovering together the Ferme Saint-Siméon (see page 34) which Monet was to paint several times. Monet stayed on the Normandy coast till the year's end, making studies for the two big submissions to the Salon that he almost certainly painted in Bazille's Paris studio, where he took temporary refuge from his financial difficulties on his return. All the while his circle of acquaintances was widening, and it is thought that he finally met Manet at the Salon in 1866, when he showed a view of the Forest of Fontainebleau and a large full-length portrait, *Camille*, which attracted the favourable attention of such influential critics as Emile Zola and Charles Blanc.

The Camille of the painting was Camille Doncieux, a model Monet seems to have met early in 1866 and who rapidly became his regular companion. She may have been the model for some (or perhaps all) of the female figures in Monet's own large *Déjeuner sur l'herbe*, in which Bazille probably modelled for most of the men. The painting was intended as Monet's main entry for the Salon of 1866, a homage to Manet and a challenge to the public, which had denounced Manet's picture of the same title three years earlier. Monet worked on it obsessively at Chailly during the spring of 1866, except when he was accidentally injured and briefly unable to paint. (Bazille profited from this by using Monet, in bandages, as the model for his *Improvised Ambulance*.) Monet continued to work on his *Déjeuner* in Bazille's studio in Paris, but for some reason it was not submitted to the Salon. Possibly it was not quite finished in time; possibly the criticism that Courbet no doubt mixed with the praise reported to Monet by Bazille discouraged him from

LEFT: **Camille: The Woman in the Green Dress, 1866**. *Emile Zola was an early champion of Monet and wrote of Camille which he saw at the Salon: 'I spotted this young woman, her long dress trailing behind, plunging into the wall as if there were a hole there... Here is a MAN among all these eunuchs'. The painting was hurriedly completed to replace Monet's unfinished Déjeuner sur l'herbe.*

RIGHT: *Study for **Déjeuner sur l'herbe, 1865-6**. Intended for the Salon of 1866, Monet's Déjeuner sur l'herbe was a homage to Manet and his controversial painting of the same title. Modelled by Monet's friends, including Camille and Bazille, it was later abandoned in lieu of rent at Argenteuil and partly destroyed.*

La Vie de Bohème

THE IDEA OF THE ARTIST as a bohemian, living on the margins of conventional, workaday society and obeying only the dictates of his own temperament, was originally an offshoot of the Romantic movement. In this conception, 'inspiration' and personal caprice were substituted for the image of the artist as a craftsman fulfilling a particular function in the social hierarchy, working for wages or specific commissions from his patrons. Thanks to the ideas of such poets and writers as Théophile Gautier and Alfred de Musset, not to mention the satire of caricaturists like Gavarni, the Romantic image of the artist was well established in France by the end of the 1840s. But it was the works of Henri Murger (or Henry Mürger as he liked to sign himself for exotic effect) that really fixed the idea in the public mind and gave the word 'bohemian' to the general vocabulary.

In his two most influential works, *La Vie de Bohème* (1849) and *Scènes de la Bohème* (1851), Murger celebrated the artists' life of freedom. Murger's artists lived in Paris, in garrets, got by in extreme poverty, which was shown as picturesque rather than grinding, and had joyous rather than squalid affairs with models and *midinettes* (shop girls). They met to smoke, drink and talk passionately until the small hours in cheap and welcoming bars and cafés in Montmartre and Montparnasse and, particularly, just across the Seine from the old city, in Saint-Germain, where the most celebrated haunt of artists and their mistresses, the Café Momus, was to be found. They were bound together by a happy camaraderie and shared their worldly goods when they had any. Prettily sad things might happen to them from time to time, but any real agony was always kept comfortably at bay.

This was just what the public wanted to hear, and Murger became one of the age's bestsellers, especially after the appearance of a dramatic version of his stories that was eventually to spawn Puccini's opera *La Bohème*. It was also what would-be artists wanted to hear, and inspired many to plunge into the troubled waters of art. Naturally, things were not really like that, as Murger was the first to recognize. Writing to a friend in 1845

LEFT: *A rare photograph of the interior of a Bal des Canotiers, or Oarsmens' Cabaret, on the Seine near Paris in the early 1860s. Monet, Renoir and other Impressionists took full advantage of the opportunities for leisure open to the new bourgeoisie in and around the capital.*

about one of his first essays in the genre, he observed ruefully, 'Whether you approve or not, I believe I've found my literary bent – in true fantasy.' All the same, there was still an element of truth, however carefully selected and arranged. And once Murger had proposed the model, life was more than ready to imitate art.

This was very much the world that Monet's generation found waiting for them when they enrolled in their various Parisian art schools towards the end of the 1850s. Murger's efforts had already brought about a number of changes. Serious artists who had frequented the Café Momus for cheapness and privacy had suddenly found themselves tourist attractions, visited by high society looking for excitement. Consequently, the centre of genuine bohemian life tended to shift very rapidly, and each new group would find or make its own. In the 1860s it was the Café Guerbois, in the avenue de Clichy on the edge of Montmartre, that the '*bande à Manet*', as they were generally known, met with their models and mistresses. Virtually all of them were having affairs with their favourite models, almost, one suspects, because it was what young, rebellious artists were supposed to do: behind this they seem to have been morally fairly conventional, and with a little more maturity Manet, Pissarro, Renoir and Monet, at least, found no difficulty in regularizing their situation by marrying the women, legitimizing any children from the relationship and settling down to a comfortable, almost bourgeois respectability.

Monet, indeed, even before he had gone through the processes of marring and legitimizing, was clearly shaping early to become the *paterfamilias* that he later became. Towards the end of 1868, before his family knew anything about his liaison with Camille, he was writting to Bazille, very sunnily for him, about how wonderfully happy he was. Monet was content to be away from Paris for the moment and living in a rented cottage in Etretat. He was out painting from nature all day and coming back at night to a cosy domestic situation with Camille and their rapidly growing child. One of his most expressive canvases of the later 1860s, *Luncheon*, shows Camille and their son Jean seated at the table, the heart, evidently, of a settled and apparently conventional family scene.

After the disruption of the Franco-Prussian War the group of artists reconstituted itself, without Monet, who had moved out of Paris, and Cézanne, who had gone back to Provence. They selected a new meeting place in Paris called the Café de la Nouvelle Athènes, which was located just round the corner from the Café Guerbois in the Place Pigalle. This group, including Monet when he was in Paris, also went to such places as the Moulin de la Galette, where they danced, and the river resort of La Grenouillère, where they boated or swam. But the Nouvelle Athènes was the real bohemian rendezvous for as long as any of them remained in any real sense bohemian. In 1886 the Irish novelist and critic George Moore recalled:

> I did not go to either Oxford or Cambridge, but I went to the Nouvelle Athènes. What is the Nouvelle Athènes? He who would know anything of my life must know something of the academy of the fine arts. Not the official stupidity you read about in the daily papers, but the real French academy, the café.

BELOW: *The Café de la Nouvelle Athènes in the rue Pigalle, Montmartre. Here the younger painters met writers and other artists, including Manet, for the lively exchange of new ideas.*

RIGHT: *A photograph of the original La Grenouillère bathing place at Chatou on the Seine near Paris. It shows the restaurant Ponton mentioned by the writer Guy de Maupassant.*

RIGHT: **Bathers at La Grenouillère, 1869.** *This rowdy pleasure spot, where the classes and sexes mingled freely, was an unusual choice of motif for Monet. It was perhaps prompted by Renoir, already a painter of the* demi-monde *of cafés and dance-halls. Renoir worked side by side with Monet as they both painted this scene.*

completing it. Whatever the reason, the picture was never shown in public, and it remained rolled up in successive studios until in the 1870s it was left as a guarantee of payment to Monet's second landlord in Argenteuil. When Monet collected it again in 1884, it had been ruined by damp, and he cut it up, preserving the central group of picnickers and a group of three standing figures to the right, including Bazille and (possibly) Camille. The composition in its entirety, Monet's most ambitious painting to date, is preserved in a smaller study in the Pushkin Museum, Moscow.

Monet had by this time met Courbet, the leading figure of the Realist movement in painting and the rebellion against academicism, and it is possible that the seated man to the left of the central group in the final version is Courbet, whom the figure much resembles. Monet had substituted this figure for the young man (probably the painter Lambron des Piltières, a fellow pupil at Gleyre's) of the study. Courbet proved to be a good friend to the young Monet, constantly encouraging him and even occasionally lending him money. This was sometimes desperately needed: Monet's critical success at the 1866 Salon had earned him money enough to move to Sèvres, where he began *Women in the Garden* — one of whom was Camille — but soon he had to flee his creditors and take refuge in Honfleur, where he continued to work on the picture and on a group of snow scenes in the neighbourhood of the Ferme Saint Siméon.

The Paris Expositions Universelles

INTERNATIONAL EXHIBITIONS were a British invention. The first real World's Fair was the Great Exhibition of 1851 in Hyde Park, occasion of the building of the Crystal Palace, which brought more than six million visitors from all over the world to admire the fruits of progress worldwide, but especially in Britain. The whole thing was conceived as a showcase for the arts and for manufactured goods, and it was spectacularly successful – so much so that the rest of the world immediately saw the usefulness of the exercise and proceeded to follow suit. France was the first, in 1855. The major point of the occasion was to establish the respectability and efficacy of the new Second Empire and Napoleon III – which it certainly did, at least with Queen Victoria, who paid a state visit to Paris during the Exposition and was delighted with what she saw. Following closely the model of the Great Exhibition, the Paris Exposition Universelle was designed as a show of arts and industries with a particular accent on the happy combination of the two. Its main innovation was the inclusion of painting.

When the time came for the next Exposition in 1867, the arts were given an especially prominent position. It was more controversial than its predecessor, where the rejection of two important paintings by Courbet from the official section of French art went more or less unremarked. The ignoring of Courbet in 1867, on the other hand, led to controversy and the setting up of a pavilion devoted exclusively to Courbet a stone's throw from the main building. Manet also had a small independent display of his own, though for the public at large neither of these outside presentations really counted for much, and even Monet was not impressed: writing to Bazille, he said that Courbet's show included an unnecessary number of horrors, and Manet's, while better (and certainly more financially successful), also contained too many bad paintings. Monet thought this the result of Manet's tendency to be swayed by flattering things other people said.

LEFT: *The Eiffel Tower still under construction on the site of the Paris Exposition Universelle.*

The 1867 Exposition marked the height of the Second Empire's glory. Already beneath the superficial glitter of the 'City of Light', which attracted more than ten million tourists that year, things were beginning to go wrong, and within three years it would all be swept away by the Franco-Prussian War. Paris was not ready for another Exposition for another twelve years. Even then, the more cautious thought that 1878 was too early to be celebrating the revival of France in a Paris whose prominent parts, such as the Tuileries palace, were still in ruins from the days of the Commune.

Seemingly the doubters were proved wrong: more than ten million visitors flocked to it and Parisians were in general ecstatic with a sense of release. The opening of the Exposition on 30 June was declared a national holiday – the first in 11 years – and Monet marked the occasion by painting two scenes of crowded streets dominated by a stunning display of flags on all the buildings. Not that this Exposition held much joy for innovative artists such as the Impressionists. The selectors for the exhibition of French art were so timid that they even completely excluded such generally accepted painters as Delacroix and Millet, leaving it to Durand-Ruel to stage a show of their work on the fringes of the Exposition. Most of the paintings that were shown followed a rather glum type of obvious storytelling – ironically, the antithesis of the carefree image that was really initiated by the 1867 Exposition.

Such an image was finally consecrated by the Exposition Universelle of 1889, and symbolized by the fair's most enduring creation,

the Eiffel Tower. The Tower's soaring edifice, in the modern material of cast-iron, must have seemed to contemporaries a 'secular cathedral' for the age of the machine. By this time the fortunes of the Impressionists had changed very considerably; Monet in particular was prominently displayed in the Exposition Centennale de l'Art Français that formed a key part of the Exposition Universelle. He had three canvases in the official show, which, given that more than 32 million admissions were recorded, must have been seen by incomparably more people than had ever seen his work before. However, in 1889 the official recognition was relatively unimportant. The main use of the Exposition was that it provided a ready-made audience for the major show, independently mounted by Georges Petit that (see page 122), presented Monet and Rodin together as the two most significant French artists of their age.

RIGHT: *A busy scene showing the unloading of goods for the Exposition of 1867. New railway networks enabled the products of the new industries to be transported easily to the site.*

In 1867 the Salon jury adopted an extremely conservative attitude, and almost everything smacking of modernity was rejected. Bazille organized a letter of protest to the Surintendant des Beaux-Arts, demanding another Salon des Refusés, that was signed by Monet, Renoir, Pissarro, Sisley and Manet, as well as such older painters as Jongkind, Charles-François Daubigny, Félix Bracquemond and probably Corot. Despite this, no notice was taken, and an attempt privately to organize a rival show to the Salon failed for lack of money. However, Monet had received enough attention to be able to show with dealers in Paris. *Women in the Garden* (clearly closely related to the abandoned *Déjeuner sur l'herbe*), after being rejected by the Salon, was bought by Bazille, who paid for it in instalments. The picture could be seen as an attempt by Monet to prove that he was a painter of figures as well as landscapes. Although Zola knew the picture and wrote approvingly of it in the following year, however, its lack of public exposure meant that it did nothing for Monet's reputation. Meanwhile, perhaps in an effort to make money, he stayed in Paris and painted a series of three pictures from the windows of the Louvre (he requested permission to do so on 27 April 1867): one looking out towards the picturesque old church of Saint-Germain l'Auxerrois and the other two representing views of more modern Paris, across the Quai du Louvre and the Jardin de l'Infante towards the distant dome of the Panthéon.

For the French in general, the principal event of 1867 was the Exposition Universelle in Paris. All over northern France industrialization was proceeding by leaps and bounds, and the trade celebrated by the Exposition was industrial as much as anything. This Exposition also included painting for the first time; Manet and Renoir painted memorable images connected with the Exposition, but Monet recorded nothing of the event.

Shortly before leaving Paris to spend the summer at Sainte-Adresse, Monet wrote one of his most revealing letters to Bazille, who had also retreated to be with his family in the south of France. He wrote about the shows Manet and Courbet had arranged privately as a response to the Salon's out-and-out rejection of their work and mentioned his Paris views, but in general he does not sound optimistic:

RIGHT: **The Terrace at Sainte-Adresse, 1867.** *Monet's family (his father is seated on the right, with possibly his aunt and a cousin beyond) are shown watching shipping from the terrace of the family home in Le Havre. The composition closely follows the Japanese style of the 'uke-oye', or 'pleasurable life', prints then popular in Paris.*

Manet's show opens in two days, and he is terribly nervous. Courbet's opens next Monday, a week today. That's a very different kettle of fish. Just think, he's inviting every artist in Paris to the opening: he's sending 3000 invitations, and in addition every artist gets a free catalogue Obviously he's doing well: he means to hold on to the building where he has already had his studio built. That's on the first floor, and next year he will hire out the room to anyone who wants to hold a show there. So we had better apply ourselves, and maybe we'll end up there, showing pictures that are beyond criticism. No more to report. Renoir and I are still at work on our Paris views. I saw Camille yesterday. I'm at my wit's end, she's ill, bedridden and penniless, or nearly, and as I have to leave on the 2nd or 3rd at the latest I must remind you that you promised to send me 80 frs at least by the first of the month.

By 25 June he was writing from Sainte-Adresse:

Did you know that before I left Paris I sold a small seascape to Cadart, and one of the Paris views to Latouche? I was so happy and relieved, as it enabled me to help poor Camille. But my dear friend, what a painful situation it is with her, all the same. She is so kind, a really good girl, and sees things very level-headedly, which makes me even sadder. On this score, I'm writing to ask you to send anything you can, the more the better. Please send it by the 1st. At the moment I'm getting on well enough with my relations, and they say I can stay here as long as I like. But they warn me that if I need any actual money I shall have to earn it. Don't let me down, will you? I have a special favour to ask of you. Camille's baby is due on July 25, and I'm going to Paris for ten days or a fortnight, and I'll need money for a lot of things. Do try and send me some extra then, if only 100 or 180 frs. Remember, without it I'll really be in difficulties.

On 8 August Camille bore him a son. It seems that Bazille did not respond with his usual alacrity, for on 12 August Monet wrote back to him from Sainte-Adresse, in evident desperation:

ABOVE: *Auguste Renoir, one of Monet's closest Impressionist friends.* These carte de visite *portraits of the group later known as the Impressionists come from Manet's own photograph album.*

BELOW: *Edgar Degas, a leading Impressionist whose style was closer to Manet's than to Monet's own.*

It's now nearly a month since I first asked you. Since then, in Paris and here, I've waited for the post every day, and every day it's the same. For the last time I'm asking you this favour. I'm going through the most awful torments. I had to come back here to keep the family happy and also because I had not enough money to stay in Paris while Camille was in labour. She has given birth to a big, beautiful boy, and in spite of everything I feel I love him. It upsets me terribly to think of his mother with nothing to eat. I was able to borrow an absolute minimum for the birth and my return trip here, but neither of us has a penny of our own.

Although Monet had, after a fashion, been reconciled with his family as a result of his success at the 1866 Salon, he had carefully avoided telling them about his Paris *ménage* with Camille. Nor did they know when the child was born. That summer, while Camille remained in Paris, Monet, in Normandy, worked on his painting *Terrace at Sainte-Adresse*, which shows the artist's family. In 1870 Monet decided to regularize his relationship with Camille and legitimize Jean. Camille and Monet were married on 28 June at the *mairie* in Paris.

The couple went for a belated honeymoon in Trouville, where Monet painted one of his most brilliant seaside pictures, of the Hôtel des Roches Noires, with all its flags flapping in the breeze. There he heard of the death of his aunt, who had so often helped him in the past. And there, too, he heard that the Emperor had declared war on Prussia. Monet, certain that he would be called up, decided to flee the country. Leaving Camille and Jean to join him later, he took ship to London.

ABOVE: *Edouard Manet, a key influence on the emerging Impressionist movement.*

BELOW: *Jean-Frédéric Bazille was a close friend and source of invaluable financial support to the young Monet.*

ARGENTEUIL: A PROVINCIAL IDYLL

THE HALF-YEAR SPENT BY MONET in London represented a low point in his life. In 1900, having returned to London again on a painting trip, he wrote to his second wife recalling 'the miserable time passed here' on his first visit and mentioning a Dr Vintras, encountered in 1870, whom he was avoiding for fear that he still owed the man money. Even though Camille and Jean soon joined him, he felt completely isolated: he did not know the language and had virtually no money. There was no prospect of help from the usual sources, since his aunt had just died. Bazille had been called up, and Monet had lost touch with him, only to learn later that he had been killed in battle with the Prussians on 28 November 1870, very shortly after Monet had arrived in London.

The news of France's defeat in the Franco-Prussian War and the fall of the Empire was followed by the even more disturbing news of the setting up and repression of the Paris Commune. One of the few bright spots in his stay in London was that Monet managed to find his way to a café frequented by exiled Frenchmen, and there he found Charles-François Daubigny, whom he had known in Paris (see page 46). Daubigny introduced him to the art dealer Paul Durand-Ruel, and through Durand-Ruel's London connections Monet was able to show his paintings in London in 1870 and 1871.

Durand-Ruel brought Monet welcome news: Pissarro was also in London, staying in Norwood,

The Franco-Prussian War

WHEN NAPOLEON III declared himself emperor in 1852 he was something of a national hero; if he was undeniably a despot, he seemed to be a fairly benevolent one. By 1870, however, his popularity at home had very much faded, and one of the principal aims of the war for him was to provide a strategy to rouse and unify patriots in resisting a supposed outside threat. The pretext for the war, in fact, was very shaky; namely, Prussia's failure to produce sufficient guarantees that the vacant throne of Spain would not be filled by a member of Prussia's own ruling house.

Some three weeks after France declared war, the German armies invaded French territory, carrying all before them. Within four months they had Paris completely surrounded, and in another two months had forced France into an ignominious armistice; Napoleon III promptly went into exile, leaving the newly formed Third Republic to sort out the ensuing mess. This was no simple matter, since during the siege of Paris the citizenry had been armed to resist the Germans, and now they refused to surrender their arms. Instead, they proclaimed the Commune, the first real socialist government in Europe, in March 1871. The new government of the Third Republic withdrew to Versailles, obtained the support of the army, and again besieged Paris. In the middle of May the final assault took place, ending in a massacre in which most of the leading Communards were shot as soon as they surrendered.

These events were fraught with significance for the Impressionists as for everyone else in Paris. Rumours flew back and forth: at one point Courbet was said to have been shot, though later this proved not to be the case. Bazille, Monet's closest friend among his fellow artists, died in battle. Some of the group, most notably Monet and Pissarro, left the country altogether during the emergency. Monet, quite simply, was liable for the draft, and he was determined not to be called up again. London was an obvious answer until the status quo was restored. For Monet, the main effect of his self-imposed exile was that in London he met Durand-Ruel, the dealer who was to be important in shaping his career for the rest of his life.

LEFT: *Defensive batteries of cannon on Montmartre in 1870, awaiting the armies of the Prussians.*
RIGHT: *Large parts of central Paris were destroyed during the bitter fighting of the war and insurrection. This photograph shows the rubble and destruction in the rue de Rivoli following the suppression of the Commune in May 1871.*

BELOW: **The Barricade** *by Edouard Manet, 1871. Manet remained in Paris and recorded the struggles of the Communards in a series of lithographs.*

near the site where the Crystal Palace from the 1851 Great Exhibition had been re-erected. The two painters made contact and visited the London galleries together. It was here that they first saw works by the English landscape painters, among them Constable and Old Crome, and discovered the paintings of Turner. At that time they would have been able to see in the National Gallery a number of important pictures from the Turner Bequest, including the two Turner himself thought the most important, *Sun Rising through Vapour* and *Dido Building Carthage*. They would also have seen *Calais Pier, Rain, Steam and Speed*, not to mention others tending towards his later, more abstract, manner. Turner's last paintings, regarded as showing a disastrous decline, were still not hung. Even so, Monet must have seen enough to confirm his own change of style, already under way, towards less decisively defined forms and an altogether freer approach to colour and the play of light through layers of mist.

The main disruption of the Commune was over by the end of May 1871, but Monet was not yet persuaded that it was wise to return directly to France. With Camille and Jean he went to Holland, a popular refuge for fleeing Communards, to the little town of Zaandam. While the months in London had not been very productive – there are only about half a dozen known works to show for the visit, all small, including his first view of *The Thames below Westminster* – he produced more paintings while in Holland. Urged on, perhaps, by Jongkind, himself Dutch, he found many congenial subjects in the watery landscapes.

Early in November 1871 Monet was back in Paris. Although he was born in Paris and had spent his most formative student years there, Monet had never really been a painter of Paris, or of urban scenes at all. All the

RIGHT: **The Train in the Snow: The Locomotive, 1875.** *The sight of the early morning train to Paris emerging out of the country mists was no doubt familiar to Monet following his move to the suburb of Argenteuil. Zola observed: 'Our artists must find the poetry of stations, just as their fathers found that of forests and flowers'.*

same, it must have been upsetting for him to find that the Tuileries Palace, adjacent to the scene of his paintings of only four years earlier, the Quai du Louvre and the Jardin de l'Infante, was now reduced to a charred ruin, soon to be swept away altogether. Ten years later the writer Jules Vallès, an exiled Communard at last permitted to return, observed of the Tuileries Gardens, 'For here, as in the Gardens of the Luxembourg, in their hours of tragedy the very flowers stank of gunpowder and blood, and the great garden was on all sides bordered with the wounded and paved with the dead.' In 1871, according to an English visitor, Edwin Child, there was 'Destruction everywhere. From the Châtelet to the Hôtel de Ville, all was destroyed.' And in 1874 a writer commenting on the Salon remarked, in the context of the war and the Commune, 'Alas, the muscle is still vibrating, the wound is still open.'

There were reasons other than merely financial ones why Monet would look for a refuge somewhere else. Since all his closest relatives were now dead (his father had died in January 1871), there was nothing to draw him back to the Normandy coast. On the other hand, there were many places just outside Paris, on the banks of the Seine, offering the desirable combination of relative cheapness, the sort of river scenes that Monet loved to paint and closeness to Paris, so that he could go in and out by train when he needed to, and could expect to be visited by his friends as they trickled back to the wrecked capital.

The answer, for the moment, was Argenteuil. Twenty-seven kilometres down the river, it was only eleven kilometres by rail, a mere quarter of an hour from the Saint-Lazare station in Paris. It was an historic town, with enough picturesque corners to appeal to a painter, and it had unspoilt countryside all around. There had always been a part of Monet that responded to nature little touched by man: back in 1868 he had written to Bazille, dismissive of the bohemian society of the Café Guerbois: 'Don't you find that one does better when all alone with nature?

LEFT: *A photograph by Marville in 1874, showing the reconstuction of the Vendome Column in Paris. Its destruction during the Commune was popularly (though wrongly) blamed on Courbet, hero of the Impressionists. When in 1873 the new government vindictively charged him with the huge cost of its re-erection, he fled France for the safety of Switzerland.*

I myself am convinced of it. I've always thought so, and regularly find that work I have done that way is better.' However, Argenteuil was a town in transition. Its proximity to Paris made it increasingly a middle-class dormitory suburb and it was already becoming industrialized when Monet arrived. In 1871 this could to some extent be ignored, the factory chimneys reduced to a minor feature smoking decoratively in the distance.

When Monet arrived with his little family, in December 1871, he first found a house to rent near the railway bridge that features in so many of his paintings, in the rue Pierre Guienne. Later he moved round the corner to the boulevard Saint-Denis. Both houses, but especially the second, were capacious for his needs, with gardens in which he would paint members of his household. The return to France seems to have unleashed a great burst of creative activity: during the first year at Argenteuil he painted more than he had altogether in the previous four years. Moreover, partly through the connection with Durand-Ruel, he was selling, and selling well. Examination of his surviving carefully kept account books for the period (he was, after all, the child of a grocer), shows that in 1872 he sold no fewer than 38 paintings, for a total of 12,100 francs. This was indeed a considerable sum given that the average annual earnings for a professional man in Paris were around 9,000 to 10,000 francs, and the average worker in Argenteuil earned in the region of 2,000 francs a year. During his six years in Argenteuil, Monet earned an average of 14,000 francs a year, which enabled him to live in a state of bourgeois grandeur.

Even at the first house in Argenteuil he always had two living-in maids, and almost certainly, considering the elaborateness of his gardens, a regular if not a full-time gardener. Although he seems to have had a running dispute with his first landlady, was always late with the rent, and wrote to Manet to borrow 50 francs of his 250 franc quarterly rent, he could in

ABOVE: *Many of the newly built railway bridges over the Seine in and around Paris were destroyed during the Franco-Prussian War, including those of Argenteuil and Chatou (shown here).*

principle afford all of this; equally, he could afford to move in June 1873 to the grander, newly built house in the boulevard Saint-Denis, which was much more expensive, with a rent of 1,400 francs a year instead of 1,000 francs. In 1872 he had made 9,850 francs from sales to Durand-Ruel alone, and in 1873 this figure increased to 19,100 francs, contributing to a total income for the year of 24,800 francs. It is difficult to avoid the conclusion that his letters complaining of poverty, his demands for loans of often trifling sums and his moans that his dealers were not paying him enough were largely a matter of habit, with the meanness of one who has known rainy days and always fears they may return. In addition, it is clear that he was extravagant and spent everything he earned.

He kept his old Paris studio until the beginning of 1875. Sisley came to visit him in Argenteuil in 1872, and side by side they painted much the same views, but most of his meetings, with Pissarro, Manet, Renoir and

RIGHT: **The Train in the Country, c. 1870–71.** *A cheerful glimpse of the Paris to Saint-Germain train in a rural scene near Bougival. Rapid suburbanization of the city environs provided a constant motif for Monet during his time at Argenteuil.*

RIGHT: **The Bridge at Argenteuil, 1874.** *One of a number of studies from this spot by the Seine in which Monet experimented with the contrast of verticals and horizontals provided by the bobbing boats and their masts offset by the bridge on its solid foundations. The whole scene is reflected in the calm of the shimmering river.*

The Impressionists and the Salon

THE GREATEST SOURCE OF DISCORD among the Impressionists during their early years was the question of what their attitude to the Salon should be. The Salon was the great official art show — indeed, the only official art show that counted — which took place each May as the climax of the spring season in Paris. It was part of a very restrictive system, centred on the Académie des Beaux-Arts, and largely the unquestioned legislator in artistic matters. The Salon was run by representatives of the Académie, who selected and rejected submissions according to the most conservative canons of taste. Official recognition was vouchsafed only if a certain artist had studied in the prescribed way at the Ecole des Beaux-Arts, or at least in the studio of a recognized painter who had done so and who upheld its principles.

When Monet arrived in Paris in the 1850s, the Académie was dominated by Ingres, a strict and particular Neo-classicist. Ingres had reduced his teaching to a series of rules concerned with finish. This could be achieved in his view only by tight formal organization and traditional draughtsmanship, learnt by endlessly copying from the masters and the drawing of objects, sculptural casts and human models with a hard clear line. There were very important — and in

their own way successful — artists who were rarely if ever allowed to exhibit at the Salon, such as Delacroix, the tempestuous Romantic, whose free, improvisatory manner of painting matched his subjects, and Courbet, the great provincial Realist.

So what were art students of the new generation to do? None of them was bent on rebellion from the outset. They all set about obtaining a correct and conventional enough training. Manet studied with one of the most successful academic painters and instructors, Thomas Couture. Degas went to the Ecole des Beaux-Arts itself. Monet, Bazille, Renoir and Sisley all met in the studio of another respectable academician, Charles Gleyre. Delacroix was finally elected to the Académie in 1857, but Ingres lived on for another ten years, and nothing looked very much like changing. In 1859, indeed, the Salon committee rejected so many pictures by important artists, including Fantin-Latour, Whistler and Manet, that the artists were incensed and showed the rejected works privately, creating something of a stir. The next year the idea was extended, with a large-scale show featuring the 'outsiders' — Delacroix, Courbet, Corot, Millet

LEFT: *Tiers of academic paintings hung closely together in a gloomy gallery of the Paris Salon of 1852.*

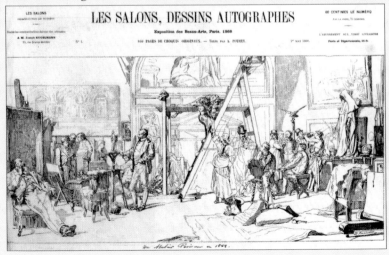

RIGHT: *A critical journal gives its view of the Salon of 1868; the illustration purports to show a typical artist's studio.*

and the Barbizon painters. The Académie closed ranks, and in 1863 the committee rejected so much that a direct appeal was made to the Emperor, who set up the Salon des Refusés, to open two weeks after the official Salon. In this any rejected artist could exhibit, if he wished, and appeal directly to the public. The *succès de scandale* of this show was Manet's *Déjeuner sur l'herbe*.

The Salon could hardly but respond to such a direct challenge, and in 1864 the committee relented. It admitted Manet, with an even more potentially scandalous painting, his defiant nude *Olympia*, as well as Degas, Pissarro, Renoir, Berthe Morisot and even Monet, whose sea and river scenes were very favourably received. This concession seemed to offer hope to the artists of breaking into the official art circuit, and confirmed the notions of some of them, Manet especially, that, however regrettably, the Salon was the only way to success, and it was necessary to keep on beating on its door to get anywhere. From 1864 until the end of the Second Empire in 1870, the Salon proved fairly unpredictable, now leaning towards new ideas, now reverting to ultra-conservatism, and the Impressionists continued to submit, usually with indifferent success.

Any hopes that the bloody end of the Second Empire in Paris and the institution of the Third Republic might mark an important change were dashed when the first revived Salon of 1872 proved to equate the restoration of order with the rejection of anything that savoured even remotely of new ideas in the arts. It was in response to this newly repressive attitude that the first independent Impressionist exhibition was staged in 1874. Not that such a relatively brief and modest showing was expected to rout the forces of the Establishment, but quite simply that some kind of alternative outlet seemed desirable, and the Exposition Artistique des Oeuvres Refusées (works refused from the Salon) in 1873 had excited an unusual amount of favourable comment. During the 1860s Monet had nurtured ambitions for success in the Salon, and painted (or at least started) a number of such ambitious works as his *Déjeuner sur l'herbe* with the Salon specifically in mind. By the early 1870s he seems largely to have given up these ambitions, but in 1880 he

ABOVE: *This engraving by Gustave Doré, entitled* The Last Day for Sending In, *mockingly depicts painting arriving at the Ecole des Beaux-Arts for submission to a Salon exhibi*tion.

decided to make a last attempt and painted two large landscapes specifically to meet what he conceived to be the Salon's requirements. One of them, *Lavacourt*, was accepted and became his first appearance in the Salon for 12 years. The other was rejected, however, and from then on Monet decided to go his own way, with the assistance of Durand-Ruel; if the Salon could do without him, he could very well do without the Salon.

others, took place in Paris. Central to all of this activity was the patronage of Durand-Ruel, who showed the work of this group of painters in Paris and staged important shows in London in 1872, 1873 and 1874.

After its enforced cessation during the Franco-Prussian War, the Commune and their aftermath, the Salon was revived in 1872. Opinion was divided among members of Monet's circle as to what their attitude towards it should be. In any case, no-one knew whether, under the new republic, a more liberal policy would be adopted. In 1872 most of the group did not even attempt to enter their work in the Salon, possibly out of loyalty to Durand-Ruel and his efforts on their behalf. The Salon proved to be as conservative as ever, however, and the 1872 protests increased in 1873 – though Manet achieved a major success there that year with the rather conventional portrait *Le Bon Bock*. So intense were the feelings that another Salon des Refusés

RIGHT: *A photograph by Frédéric Boissonas of girls in a poppy field. Monet was to paint this charming subject, evocative of lazy summer afternoons, many times over the next few years.*

RIGHT: **Poppies near Vétheuil, 1880**. *The poppy field was an important motif in Monet's work throughout his years at Argenteuil, Vétheuil and Giverny. This interesting view sets the poppy landscape firmly in the shadow of the expanding town.*

was hurriedly organized, the Exposition Artistique des Oeuvres Refusées. In this more liberal context Renoir in particular commanded favourable notice, but it was clearly time that the rejected and independent-minded artists did something more positive to help themselves establish a separate artistic identity and presence.

Hence arose the idea of staging their own show, if necessary in open rivalry to the Salon. Monet seems to have been the most determined and enthusiastic of them, while Pissarro, ever practical and diplomatic, was the organizing intelligence. On 27 December 1873 a document was drawn up setting up a type of joint stock company, to which all participating artists would contribute equally. It was signed by Monet, Pissarro, Degas (with some reservations), Renoir, Sisley and Morisot. Pictures would be hung initially by size, and then by drawing lots. Premises were provided by the photographer Nadar, off the boulevard des Capucines. Other artists, including Boudin, were persuaded to exhibit, and 165 works by 30 artists were assembled. Only Manet refused to join in, on the grounds that such a show prejudiced their chances of winning future entry to the Salon. The show opened on 15 April 1874, for one month.

Monet was represented in the show by five oil paintings and seven pastel sketches. One of the oils, *Impression, Sunrise*, painted on a visit to Le Havre in 1872, produced interesting repercussions. Most of such critics as deigned to notice the show either made jokes or were dismissive, one of the most hostile being Louis Leroy of the satirical magazine *Le Charivari*. He made use of the title of the picture to allege that the painters represented in the show were capable of producing only 'impressions', not finished paintings, and in the heading of his article the term 'Impressionists' was coined to label and deride them. The group discovered that the best way of turning the insult was to adopt it with pride, and from then on their artistic movement became known as the 'Impressionists'.

In most practical terms the first Impressionist exhibition was disastrous. Few pictures were sold, little critical credit gained and at the end of the year the company's accounts showed it to

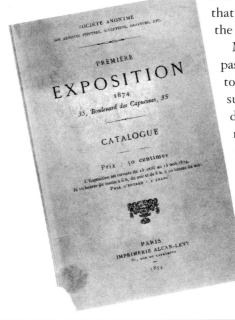

BELOW: *The catalogue of the first group show of the Impressionists, mounted in defiance of the official Salon at the photographer Nadar's studio in 1874. The artists formed a Société Anonyme, or Limited Company, for the purpose.*

be in debt. At this point it was dissolved, by unanimous consent. The bonds of friendship still remained strong, however, and in the summer of 1874 Manet and Renoir spend some time with Monet at Argenteuil, often painting together. From this visit dates Manet's *Claude Monet in his Studio-Boat*, which shows Monet and Camille in a boat, under an awning, he seated at an easel at work on a sunny river scene. (Daubigny, another *plein-air* painter, also used a boat as a studio when working on the rivers of France.) It is clear from this picture that Monet and Renoir, by their example and their overwhelming enthusiasm, had gone a long way towards converting Manet to their doctrine of *plein-air* painting and a much looser, more fluid, use of paint.

In and around Argenteuil Monet painted prolifically, both summer and winter – although the most familiar of his works from this period are the bright and sunny ones, there are also many wonderful scenes of snow and grey weather. He was one of the most successful exhibitors in the second group show, which took place at Durand-Ruel's gallery and for the first time made a small profit overall. At least one of Monet's paintings on

LEFT: *A small inn at Asnières on the banks of the Seine displays canoes available for hire. Boating on the river was a popular weekend pastime for Parisians and a subject painted by most of the Impressionists.*

Japonisme

WESTERNERS HAD BEEN interested in things oriental since the early seventeenth century, when blue-and-white porcelain from China, along with tulips from Turkey, became the height of fashion. Examples of Japanese prints made their way west in the early nineteenth century, mainly as curiosities, and by 1880 the illustrator Félix Bracquemond had the first representative Western collection. But such interests took a different turn in the 1880s, when the first examples of the Japanese colour woodblock print made their appearance in Paris and London in considerable numbers, allegedly first as the disregarded wrapping paper for other things. Artists rapidly became fascinated with them, partly no doubt because of the romance and mystery of Japan, completely closed to outsiders for two centuries and only finally penetrated again by the American Commodore Perry in 1853. But even more potent than such nebulous ideas was the bizarreness, by Western standards, of the prints themselves, embodying a completely different notion of perspective, proportion and composition from anything previously known in the West.

Monet was very early a collector of Japanese prints: he stated late in life that he bought his first in 1856, when he was just 16, and through the years he assembled a very distinguished collection, much of which is on show today in his house at Giverny. For a while, during the 1870s in particular, collectors were

obsessed with everything Japanese – fans, lacquer, blue-and-white china as well as prints. The more superficial aspects of this vogue can be seen in Monet's painting, exhibited in the second Impressionist show of 1876 as *Japonnerie* and later know as *La Japonaise* (with evident inaccuracy, since the blonde model, in no way Japanese, is in fact his wife Camille).

The influence of Japanese art went much deeper than would be suspected from this one picture. In 1867, when he painted *Terrace at Sainte-Adresse*, a view of the Channel across the garden of his family's summer retreat, he referred to it as 'my Chinese painting with flags in it'. There are in fact close parallels between the treatment of space and perspective and a number of Japanese prints he must have known or even owned. Monet does the same slightly strange things with perspective as Hokusai might, constructing his scene in bands that appear to run parallel – the edge of the garden, the fence, the horizon with its assorted ships – and repressing or distorting most of the evidence of recession. Not only is this a very Japanese manner of framing a sea-scene, but also it emphasizes the presentation of pictorial space as a stage upon which people and objects can be disposed with an informal but aesthetically satisfying balance.

Two woodblock prints by Hokusai which directly inspired Monet; he owned a considerable collection of Japanese art, still to be seen at Giverny. It has been suggested that Hokusai's Thirty-six Views of Mount Fuji *gave Monet the idea of painting in series from the same motif.*

The principal effect of Japanese prints on Western artists was not so much one of encouraging direct emulation as of retooling all their responses to the world around them, and their ideas of what did and did not make a satisfactory picture. Other Impressionists, such as Caillebotte and Degas, were influenced in this deeper, more far-reaching way. Caillebotte clearly learned the value of some of the more daring viewpoints in his pictures from Japanese practice, and Degas threw off the shackles of his formal education to construct his pictures with a daring but effective asymmetry, outbalancing the woman he is painting by an enormous vase of flowers in the centre of the canvas or letting his figures walk boldly in and out of frame as though it were a casually selected slice of life.

This kind of influence was strongly present in Monet, making his choice of landscape subjects and even unconsciously dictating the sort of thing he would find it interesting to look at with an artist's eye. During his famous storm-tossed stay on the Breton island of Belle-Ile, he painted a number of rock formations that would hardly have appealed to anyone not steeped in oriental landscape art, with its particular appreciation of the strange effects of wind and water on the raw material of landscape (see page 100). Shortly afterwards, in Antibes, the Japanese aesthetic had much to do with the precise way a solitary tree was placed on the canvas. The constituents of the water garden that he spent most of his latter years creating and painting were nearly all derived from Japanese art – not only the Japanese bridge, an obvious picturesque touch, but also the choice of water-lilies, irises and bamboo as the most important plants. What he was eventually to do artistically with the water-lilies was also definite-ly oriental. The delight with which he followed the random fluid patterns they made on the water, and the screen-like effect of his series of *Grandes Décorations*, the great panoramic semi-abstractions that were to end up in the Orangerie of the Tuilerie created pictures from the floating world indeed.

RIGHT: **Camille in Japanese Costume (*La Japonaise*), 1876**
Monet put Camille in a blonde wig to paint this extraordinary costume piece in an effort to repeat his Salon success of 1866.

show there, the female figure in oriental costume entitled *Japonnerie* (later known inaccurately as *La Japonaise*, it depicts Camille in a Japanese theatrical costume), attracted a great deal of attention and sold for a high price. Possibly it owed this success to its relatively conventional nature; it could almost have been devised with the Salon in mind, though it is the last of Monet's works to permit that idea. Monet's degree of commercial success at this time is indicated by the fact that, of the 17 of his landscapes on show, nine had already been sold, and were lent back to the exhibition by the opera singer Jean Baptiste Faure.

The serious critics were now beginning to take notice. Three literary figures who sometimes functioned as art critics, Edmond Duranty, Emile Zola and Stephane Mallarmé, wrote about the painters at length and in general favourably, though each tended to stress the political implications of their work and its relation to Realism rather than the technical innovations. Duranty, in fact, wrote the first book about the Impressionists, under the title *La nouvelle peinture* (1876). An article by Zola was written for Russian readers of a journal published in St Petersburg. They were informed that Monet was 'unarguably the head of the group' and left to mull over Zola's judgment that:

Without doubt we are seeing the birth of a new school. Here there is a revolutionary ferment that little by little will prevail over the Académie des Beaux-Arts itself, and in 20 years will have transformed the Salon from which these innovators are now excluded.

ABOVE: *The first edition of the* Impressionist Journal, *6 April 1877. The group mounted a defence of their work in response to a hostile press, led by* Le Figaro.

Mallarmé, for the English readers of *The Art Monthly Review* in London, invented a 'typical' Impressionist, who gave as his credo:

I content myself with reflecting on the clear and durable mirror of painting ... [when I am] rudely thrown at the close of an epoch of dreams in the front of reality. I have taken from it only that which properly belongs to my art.

All the same, such detailed and intelligent consideration showed how far taste had moved even since 1874. The scope and variety of the Paris reviews was also significant, although favourable reviews were still outnumbered by hostile ones. Still, notice was notice, and the Impressionists were definitely a talking-point.

Monet was also involved in the next, ill-judged group enterprise: an auction of the group's pictures that took place at the Hôtel Drouot in Paris later in 1876. Altogether 72 pictures by Monet, Renoir, Sisley and Morisot were offered for sale. Many remained unsold and the prices for those that did sell were mostly derisory. Monet was not particularly abashed by this reverse: he was benefitting from Durand-Ruel's continuing support and from the enthusiasm of a number of individual patrons. The group as a whole had attracted the interest of several prosperous men. Whereas Faure was particularly dedicated to Monet, Victor Chocquet's preference was first and foremost for Paul Cézanne, although it embraced the rest of the Impressionists, including Monet. Gustave Caillebotte was a rather different case: an engineer with a talent for painting, he was for a while a neighbour of Monet at Argenteuil, and took part in several of the communal painting expeditions. He bought several key works by Monet and other of the Impressionists, exhibited in five of the eight Impressionist group shows and was invaluable as an organizer.

Caillebotte it was who organized the third show, delayed until April 1877 because of the disastrous results of the auction. It took place just down the street from Durand-Ruel's gallery and was for the first time officially labelled 'Impressionist'. It was arranged at an exclusive dinner-party given by Caillebotte and attended by Degas, Monet, Renoir, Sisley, Manet and Pissarro as well as Caillebotte himself. Already by this time the critical tide was turning, and Caillebotte's plans were carefully thought out in terms of the overall image presented as well as the works shown. Monet was represented by 30 works, only nine of them unsold before the start of the show and four of them part of the great series showing the interior of the Saint-Lazare station, which must have been hot off the easel.

ABOVE: *An affectionate sketch of Monet at work in his bush hat by Edouard Manet, with whom he frequently painted on and around the river at Argenteuil in 1874, sometimes from Monet's famous studio boat.*

ABOVE: **The Red Cape,** c.1868-70. *A charming vision of Camille passing the window at Etretat, appearing as a flash of warmth in the wintery light. This was one of the very few early works that Monet kept until his death.*

Monet's letters of the period are much as usual — full of appeals for money, protestations of penury and invitations larded with references to the humble conditions and simple meals those invited would have to expect if they came. All this can be taken with a large pinch of salt. But few of the paintings in the 1877 show were of Argenteuil and perhaps Monet was becoming restive. At the beginning of his time there he presented the surroundings as idyllic: quaint, countrified and unspoilt. We know from other sources that such a view on Monet's part was highly selective. Throughout his six-year residence the town was growing apace, as more and more people commuted from Paris. Sometimes Monet painted areas of new building, but generally in such a way that the changes are not visible. *The Houses at the Edge of the Field* is of a summer field, full of poppies and other flowers, the sky of broken clouds. Only on more careful consideration do we observe that the three-and-a-half houses in the middle distance appear to be unfinished, with gaping spaces where the doors and windows will be. But they are not presented as an intrusion; rather as an already established, comfortable part of the landscape. And after all, Monet himself was living in a house that in reality was scarcely older than those in the painting.

Monet does sometimes seem to have remembered his self-appointed mission as a young man to be a 'painter of modern life'. However the picture *Unloading Coal* remains exceptional, if not unique, in his work: Monet himself described it to Durand-Ruel some years later as 'a solitary note' among his paintings. It is the only painting by Monet in which he directly approached the modern industrial world and sought to depict its toll on

LEFT: **Camille at the Window, Argenteuil, 1873.** *Another souvenir of Monet's early married life is this delightful scene of Camille surrounded by flowers.*

ABOVE: *The river at Bougival, where Monet lived in 1868 and 1869, when he painted the nearby La Grenouillère. Renoir, Pissarro and Berthe Morisot also lived and painted here from time to time.*

humanity. It is also clear, as he observed the laden men precariously carrying bags of coal on narrow gang-planks across the river mud of a Paris suburb, in a sinister half-light, that he disliked what he saw.

In the mid 1870s the garden seems to have become a symbol of Monet's withdrawal from the modern world. Already in the 1860s he had painted a number of garden pictures, usually fig-ure subjects with an attractive garden setting. At Argenteuil they became primarily garden pictures, with any figures shown in intimate community with the landscape. Presumably the garden of Monet's second home in Argenteuil was large, rambling and deliber-ately informal. Indeed, except for the titles, there is no indication that the woodland scenes *In the Garden* and *Camille with a Parasol in the Garden* are set in a garden at all, or that the setting of *Camille in the Grass* is not a meadow. A couple of views of the garden from the house give a more realistic idea of the garden's size and geography, but it comes as a sur-prise to encounter Renoir's much more down-to-earth image of *Monet Working in his Garden at Argenteuil*, which makes it clear as none of Monet's paintings does how close the unromantic suburban world of bourgeois houses and their neat little gardens crowded in. It was a world Monet could exclude, but only by a conscious effort.

From painting all over Argenteuil, Monet retreated, by the beginning of 1876, to painting only in his garden. The element of escaping from the constant encroachments of urban, even metropolitan, life seems to be strongly present. His work for two new patrons underlines this. Through Cézanne he finally met Cézanne's patron Chocquet, and in the spring of 1876 he returned to painting Paris in four pictures of the Tuileries gardens from the balcony of Chocquet's apartment in the rue de Rivoli. Again, the choice seems to be significant: he concentrated on the greenery and ignored the bustling street below, as well as the still-ruined Tuileries palace. Later the same year he accepted an invitation from Ernest Hoschedé, a wealthy business man who was an early collector of Impressionist work, to visit his château at Montgeron, up the Seine from Paris. Monet was commissioned by Hoschedé to paint for it four decorative panels.

The visit to Hoschedé represented a definite psychological move away from the town and by implication the modern world. The situation at Hoschedé's Château de Rottenbourg was certainly very tempting. It was on the edge of deep, lush countryside. The lifestyle of Hoschedé, a Paris fabric tycoon, was luxurious for host and guest alike. The château had a studio in which Monet could work, a retreat in the midst of a virtually untouched rural environment where Monet was free to shut himself away. He stayed there from August until December, with brief visits to Argenteuil, where he painted some of his most unconditionally idyllic local views, making Argenteuil look as much like Montgeron as he was able.

LEFT: *A contemporary view of Argenteuil from the popular journal* L'Illustration *in 1869. Like other resorts on the Seine, it was becoming very popular with Parisians at weekends.*

RIGHT: **Men Unloading Coal, 1875.** *The industrialized present and its new working class was an unusual subject for Monet. This highly stylized treatment of workers carrying coal from a barge beneath the iron bridge at Asnières emphasizes through its symmetry their loss of individuality in the back-breaking task.*

RIGHT: **Gare St Lazare: Arrival of a Train, 1877.** *Annoyed by critics' inability to see the point of painting a subject in fog, Monet left his idyllic garden for Paris in 1877 to record the dramatic visual phenomenon of a Paris railway station. Renoir recollected his saying: 'I'll get them to delay the train to Rouen for half an hour. The light will be better then'. 'You're mad', Renoir replied; but Monet, presented his card to the director, who obligingly halted the train.*

Unexpectedly, right in the middle of what amounted to a love affair with nature, Monet took an apartment in Paris in January 1877 to work on a series of pictures in and around the Saint-Lazare station. This group of paintings, a dozen in all, seem to be a celebration of industrial romanticism, the dominating power of the great engines belching smoke and steam, the grand scale of the great cast-iron and glass roof arching over all. The simplest of them, *Gare Saint Lazare: The Signal* (see page 95) expresses this most markedly: at the time, one of Monet's critics found the disk of the signal in the centre foreground 'menacing,' and there is undoubtedly that element in all the pictures, even when allied to a sheer sensuous appreciation of the play of light through vapour and the iridescent colours of the station interior.

Part of Monet's intention in his choice of subject may also have been a consciousness of his audience and the desirability, as he remarked in a letter to the critic Théodore Duret requesting the loan of a picture, of being able 'to exhibit myself under various aspects' in the group show that took place in 1877.

Even though financially 1877 was his best year since 1873, with his earning 15,177 francs, he was still complaining of poverty. He had accumulated debts as a result of his own improvidence. Camille was pregnant a second time, and the pregnancy was not going well. He wrote desperately to his friend and doctor, Georges de Bellio, begging him to buy 25 works for a mere 500 francs. There were other complications, too. During his time in Montgeron Monet may have begun a romantic involvement with Hoschedé's wife Alice. Then, in August, Hoschedé was declared bankrupt. One day he vanished from home without explanation, and the next his wife knew was conveyed in a frantic letter from Belgium, where a friend had taken him in after foiling a suicide attempt:

My beloved wife, how else can I address you, or will you still allow me to address you? I have fought like a giant for the last month ... I've lost my head ... and wanted to kill myself ... Being in Paris is no longer possible for me. Ought I to go on living for you and the children I worship? Don't curse me ... Tell me to have the courage to continue, or to disappear ... Above all, let no one try to see me, or I shall kill myself.

Since about half of Monet's income for the year that had come directly from Hoschedé, the ruin of the tycoon meant more to Monet than just the disappearance of the Château de Rottenbourg as a kind of paradise.

No doubt the air of agitation and menace that has been seen in Monet's last important Argenteuil painting, *Argenteuil: The Bank in Flower*, comes as much from his personal circumstances as from his feelings about the

ABOVE: *A photograph showing passengers waiting for a train to the suburbs in the Gare St Lazare, Paris. The developing railway enabled former Parisians to commute between Paris and the rural villages along the Seine, in addition to visiting as weekend tourists.*

changes taking place in Argenteuil. A recent commentator has found the picture 'tranquil ...like a nineteenth-century response to Watteau's *Embarkation for the Island of Cythera*'. To most, however, the sulphurous pall hanging over the town and factories in the distance and the overbearing, aggressive-coloured flowers in the foreground seem to reflect his discomfort, while the composition, with the flowered bank and the garden fence in the foreground, seems to suggest a permanent cutting-off of painter and spectator alike from the once-loved town.

In January 1878 the Monets left Argenteuil for good, moving back temporarily to Paris. In March Camille gave birth to a second son, Michel, but remained very ill. When the new Exposition Universelle opened in June, Monet was still in Paris and marked the occasion by painting twin pictures of the fluttering flags in the rue Montorgueil. In the show of French painting that formed part of the Exposition even the older and more conservative painters such as Millet, Delacroix and Théodore Rousseau were considered unsafe and were cold-shouldered. Durand-Ruel staged a show of the Impressionists' work in opposition to the official choice and achieved no success with it, critical or commercial. Clearly another group exhibition was for the moment out of the question.

With all the doors apparently closed to him, what was Monet to do? For reasons of economy as well as in the search for new scenes to paint, he decided to plunge himself into the countryside and moved for the summer down-river to the still unspoilt town of Vétheuil, 12 kilometres from the nearest railway station. He found the place 'ravishing' and his family was soon joined by another, in almost as rocky a financial situation: Monet, his wife and two children found themselves sharing the same modest house with Ernest Hoschedé, now back from Belgium and virtually penniless, and Alice and their six children. It was very different from Montgeron, but at least it was a refuge of sorts and a home.

ABOVE: *A brief sketch of the station interior from one of Monet's notebooks, which he used on the spot to fix the elements of his compositions.*

VÉTHEUIL: THE WANDER YEARS

LEFT: **Ice Floes, 1880.**
Following Camille's painful death after a long illness in 1879, Monet painted a number of river views near Vétheuil imbued with the lifeless icy chill of winter. Huysmans called this oil 'intensely melancholic'.

THERE IS A DEFINITE SENSE of renewal, relaxation and freedom in the first images Monet recorded at Vétheuil. On his arrival he began painting with a speed and intensity he had not known for six or seven years. At 38 he was at the height of his energies, in full maturity. Between settling there and leaving in 1880 he painted at least 178 substantial canvases, nearly all done within a mile of his home.

The Seine was in constant use as a route for freight, carried by barges and tugs plying between Paris and the coast, but Monet deliberately turned his back on these signs of an industrial world beyond the protecting countryside, and the river is nearly always presented as deserted, save for the odd rowing boat. Indeed, even the town itself, small and unspoilt as it was, seems to have been something he preferred to shun and present almost always as a distant prospect.

Throughout the first year in Vétheuil, Camille was little more than an invalid. Hoschedé was away for more and more of the time, presumably trying by whatever means he could to restore some of his fortune, without success. Alice, like Camille, had a baby to look after, as well as five other children, and when the Hoschedés' nursemaid and governess deserted them, leaving only the cook, she had to take practical charge of the whole household.

Then, in September 1879, Camille died. To judge from Monet's letters to the doctor Georges de Bellio, it must have come as a happy release, since she had been sinking and in constant pain for some time. On 17 August Monet had written asking for money and saying that he could not work because he could not afford to buy paints; he was also too distraught to paint: 'At the moment it is having to see my wife's life constantly under

ABOVE: *A photograph of Monet in about 1880, at the time of his unconventional* ménage *with Alice Hoschedé, first at Vétheuil and then at Poissy.*

threat that terrifies me, and I find it unbearable to watch her suffering so much and be unable to do anything to help.' On 5 September he wrote again to de Bellio to announce her death, asking him to retrieve a locket from pawn in Paris as he wished to place it round Camille's neck before she was buried. On the 26th he wrote to his friend Pissarro thanking him for his letter of condolence: 'You, more than anyone, must know something of my affliction.' He was frantic with grief and did not know where to turn for help in looking after his two young children. 'I am much to be pitied, for I am very pitiable.'

It was natural that in due course he should turn to Alice Hoschedé. There seems to be no doubt that he had been devoted to Camille and was genuinely devastated when she died. She had come from a poor family and was still in her teens when he met her first. Monet's early paintings of Camille suggest a considerable physical allure. She was, indeed, the quintessential first love of a man destined to go far. Alice Hoschedé, when they first met in Montgeron, must have represented something very different to Monet. Her background was the opposite of Camille's. Born Alice Raingo, she was an heiress. Her dowry considerably augmented Ernest Hoschedé's short-lived fortune, while the Château de Rottenbourg was inherited from her father. She was brought up to riches and surrounded by art, a state of affairs that was if anything intensified by her marriage to Hoschedé. She was three years older than Camille, married to Hoschedé for 13 years and already the mother of five children with another expected when she and Monet had first met. Her charms would have been altogether different, involving maturity, sophistication and poise.

She had been nursing Camille through her last illness and looking after Camille's two children along with her own. She was the woman of the house, and Monet, given Ernest Hoschedé's long absences, was the man of

ABOVE: *Alice Hoschedé in the late 1870s. Still married to Ernest at this time, she appears as a finely dressed wife of the* haute bourgeoisie.

the house, if only by default. Despite the socially unconventional situation, it seemed only reasonable that they should make common cause, and pool their families and resources. Initially there were no adverse comments on their curious *ménage*: probably Hoschedé was there frequently enough to keep up appearances, and in any case in Vétheuil they were remote from Paris society and Parisian gossip. Hoschedé's attitude remains mysterious. Apparently he had taken up the life of a bachelor in Paris, and more or less abandoned his wife and children. On the other hand, the Hoschedé children remembered at least one confrontation later on when Hoschedé demanded that Alice return to him with the children, and though the eldest, Marthe, sided with her father, Alice was adamant in her refusal.

During the first years at Vétheuil, Monet was developing his 'Impressionist' style, applying it to a strictly limited range of motifs. De Bellio, answering Monet's desperate request for financial help penned on 17 August, when Camille appeared to be dying, replied dryly:

> I must tell you, as frankly as I can (and you know I can be very frank) that you cannot possibly hope to make money with paintings that look so unfinished. You are caught, dear friend, in a vicious circle from which I can see no escape. To make money you have to have paintings to sell; to be able to paint them you have to have money.

In a review of the fourth Impressionist show, which took place from April to May 1879, the usually admiring Zola told his Russian readers, probably referring to the Vétheuil pictures, that Monet seemed 'worn out with too hurried production. He is satisfied with what just gets by. He is looking at nature with the passionate intensity of a true creator.'

Monet had been detaching himself more and more from the Parisian art scene. He participated in the 1879 Impressionist show only because Caillebotte insisted and obligingly advanced him 2,500 francs. He did not go to Paris to help prepare the show and did not visit it while it was on. Caillebotte had complete responsibility for assembling the 41 canvases by Monet that were included, borrowing 29 of them from private collections to go with 12 new works. Some of the borrowed pictures went back as far as the *Terrace at Sainte-Adresse* of 1867, or further, so that Monet's section constituted a retrospective exhibition on a small scale. After Camille's death he cut himself off even more completely from the outside world. For the first

three months, it seems, he never went out of the house and concentrated on still-lifes of game, flowers and fruit. These paintings may well have been more readily saleable than his 'unfinished' landscapes. By the time he was ready to go out again, the countryside was in the grip of an unusually severe winter. The frozen landscape is thought by some to have assumed a special significance for him in his grief-stricken state.

Monet felt that it was time to take his career in hand, and as well as painting small, brilliantly sketchy and light-saturated pictures of snow and ice, he set about producing two large, evidently 'finished', pictures specifically to have another attempt at being accepted by the Salon. It was the first time he had tried since 1868, and he clearly considered carefully what he was doing. He wrote to the sympathetic critic Théodore Duret:

I am hard at work on three large pictures, two of them destined for the Salon and the third too much to my own taste to submit, since it would certainly be rejected; I must clearly do something more sober and bourgeois ... I'm not doing this because I want to, but since it must be done, here goes!

In the event, the Salon accepted one of the pictures, a relatively conventional view of Lavacourt, the hamlet just across the river from Vétheuil, and rejected the bolder and bleaker *Ice-floes. Lavacourt* attracted some favourable

LEFT: **The Artist's Garden at Vétheuil, 1880.**
A charming view of the garden at Vétheuil, where the Monet and Hoschedé couples had set up home with their eight children. Ernest spent much time in Paris, and, following Camille's death, Monet and Alice were left to support one another.

RIGHT: **Hoarfrost near Vétheuil (*Le Givre*), 1880.**
The gradual thaw in Monet's grief was increasingly reflected by a new freedom and experimentation in his work.

1880 Claude Monet

attention, though not enough, he knew, to lead to the kind of sales he hoped for. From then on Monet gave up all ideas of exhibiting at the Salon. He had to find other ways of developing his career.

At about this time he first had the opportunity to give interviews. It is interesting to note that much of what he said was misleading in its implications or downright untrue. He was probably the first artist with a modern understanding of the importance of projecting an intriguing image, even at the cost of bending the truth. The first major opportunity of this kind came in June 1880, when he accepted an invitation from the publisher Georges Charpentier to hold a one-man exhibition in a gallery attached to his smart magazine *La Vie Moderne*.

Obviously it was understood from the start that this would make news for the magazine, which would support and publicize Monet as a provocative figure. Duret was enlisted to help organize the show and write the introduction to the catalogue, much of it written to Monet's dictation, and there was also an extensive interview in *La Vie Moderne* by one of the staff reporters, Emile Taboureux. Monet showed 18 works in the exhibition, which was on at the same time as the Salon. Degas was disgusted, regarding such personal publicity as vulgar. (It was of course easy enough for Degas, with a comfortable private income, to take this line.) The publicity it gained Monet was the beginning of the Monet legend, created and fostered by himself. The most important part of it, and the one that still shapes suppositions about Monet today, was his insistence, in both interview and catalogue introduction, that he painted entirely on the spot, in the open air. He even went so far, in the interview, as to say that he had never had a studio and could not 'understand how any painter can shut himself up in a room. To draw, yes, but certainly not to paint.' Indicating the landscape around, he concluded dramatically, 'This is my studio.' It was not true; he had certainly always had a studio, even if at times as rudimentary as an attic bedroom, and although he generally began his paintings or made sketches for them in the open air, he almost invariably worked them up and completed them indoors, often over quite a long period.

The truth was insufficiently colourful, too similar to the way academic painters worked. It suited Monet to appear as the romantic rebel, the untrammelled genius working directly under the inspiration of the moment. In the reaction against the constraints of academic painting that was coming in the 1880s, this made him something of a hero and a rallying point. Although in private he sometimes admitted to the amount of calculation and sheer hard work that made his pictures what they were, in public he maintained the fiction of painting only *en plein air* until well after 1900, by which time his age seemed to excuse him the worst rigours of his legendary battles with the elements. The fanciful account of his creative process helps to explain his increasing isolation from Parisian art circles, distracting commentators (some of whom, like Zola, had already started hinting broadly at the truth) from creating a scandal over his irregular relationship with Alice Hoschedé.

Their *ménage* really became an issue in December 1880, when he and Alice and their eight children moved from Vétheuil to nearby Poissy, about half-way between Vétheuil and Argenteuil. The official reason for the move was that it was necessary for the schooling of the older children, but it meant severing the last apparent link with Ernest Hoschedé, and left whatever vestiges of bourgeois respectability the household still retained

RIGHT: **The Studio Boat, 1876.** *Dense foliage is reflected in the water and flanks the onlooker watching the floating 'studio', a type of local punt with a cabin attached. Monet created the studio so that he could choose his viewpoint when painting the river.*

RIGHT: **The Seine at Vétheuil, 1880-82.** *A tranquil early summer scene near Monet's home reveals the artist's growing contentment with his surroundings. Following his move along the river to Poissy with Alice in 1880, his irregular domestic arrangements forced him to forego society and to live increasingly within his family circle.*

in tatters. As if to emphasize his detachment from his old associates, Monet did not take part in the fifth and sixth Impressionist exhibitions, in 1880 and 1881, and was lured back only briefly for the seventh in 1882 at the urging of Caillebotte, Pissarro and Durand-Ruel. (This show offered an opportunity for Monet to exhibit *Ice-floes*, the picture rejected at the 1880 Salon, and *Setting Sun*, painted at the same time but judged to be too much to his own taste for acceptance.) Since 1880 he had been bent on taking his own line, with one-man shows and Durand-Ruel dealing on his behalf.

In fact 1880 showed a considerable upturn in Monet's financial fortunes. That year he earned just under 14,000 francs, and the next, partly no doubt because his arrangement with Durand-Ruel had been sorted out with a contract for regular advances against purchase, the figure was up to more

Durand-Ruel and the Impressionist Market

UNTIL THE 1860s THE art dealer as such hardly existed; there were dealers in prints and antiques, who might also carry paintings by artists of the past, and there were artists' colourmen, who might display the occasional contemporary painting in their windows and build up a stock of such works by taking pictures from artist-customers in exchange for the materials they sold. Few if any had space for exhibiting art: if any passers-by were interested by a work in the window, they could pull out others, one at a time, from stock. It was widely felt that customers would be confused and put off by seeing a number of canvases together.

The Salon in Paris was at this time the most significant official art show, and it held enormous influence over the French art market. Selection for a Salon exhibition, therefore, represented the height of any would-be artist's ambitions, and his best chance of commercial success, but the strictness of selection requirements was limiting, and there were many artists, even quite distinguished ones, who seldom or never had their work accepted. The nineteenth century saw the development of a new bourgeois audience for art, who were ready and able to buy pictures from artists smaller than the giants favoured by the Salon. This development prompted the need for a means of purchasing works other than at the Salon or by direct purchase from the artist's studio. This is where dealers such as Paul Durand-Ruel came in.

Durand-Ruel's father had followed a familiar route from stationer to artists' colourman, and from there to a sideline in selling pictures. When Paul took over the business in 1865, it was still primarily dealing in artists' materials, and it was his decision in 1869 to concentrate entirely on selling pictures. His father had established a particular connection with the group of sober landscape painters associated with Barbizon; it was through one of them, Charles-François Daubigny, that Paul Durand-Ruel first met Monet in London during his period of exile.

Durand-Ruel's practice was the normal one of buying paintings outright

LEFT: *A photograph of Monet's dealer Paul Durand-Ruel by Dornac, taken around 1910. He was to have extensive, though not exclusive, representation of Monet's work from 1880 onwards.*

RIGHT: *A cartoon by Draner from the satirical magazine* Le Charivari, *originally entitled 'A Visit to the Impressionists', 1882. The cartoonist mocks what he sees as the sheer ugliness of the paintings in the group show. Such recurrent ridicule still made works difficult to sell.*

from the artist and subsequently reselling them. He immediately bought some pictures from Monet. Later, back in France, Monet's correspondence from Argenteuil is sprinkled with cries for help, which was usually provided. As the 1870s progressed, this help often took the form of advances on promised work as well as the direct purchase of work in hand. Durand-Ruel had the same relationship as patron-cum-dealer with other Impressionists. In 1921 Monet told an interviewer, 'Without him we would have starved to death . . . We owe him everything.'

It is not altogether clear how beneficial the arrangement was for Durand-Ruel at the beginning. The first Monet he showed was *The Entrance to Trouville Harbour*, evidently one of the canvases that Monet had taken with him to London, in a New Bond Street show of miscellaneous French works he organized in December 1870. He continued to show Monet in London and Paris throughout the decade, although to begin with it seems to have been largely an act of faith. His patronage came and went somewhat depending on his financial situation. In 1872 and 1873 he bought paintings from Monet to the tune of 29,000 francs, but in 1874, hit by a downturn in the national economy, he had to retrench. The first Impressionist exhibition took place in borrowed premises just down the road from his gallery, but the second and third, in 1876 and 1877, took place in his premises between the rue Laffitte and the rue Le Peletier.

In 1880 Durand-Ruel arrived at a regular arrangement with Monet by which Monet would receive advances in exchange for Durand-Ruel's having first call on the work done. This was a near as he ever got to the arrangement ideally he would have liked with all his artists, an exclusive representation. Unfortunately, in 1882 the bank that was his main backer, the Union Générale, crashed, and his activities had to be reduced for some years. Monet supported him in general terms, and they remained close friends, but by this time Monet was willing to do business with other dealers and sometimes play them against one another, as well as negotiating most of his important sales himself, directly with the collector.

The connection with Durand-Ruel was still important to him, however, if only in terms of public exposure. Since Durand-Ruel was

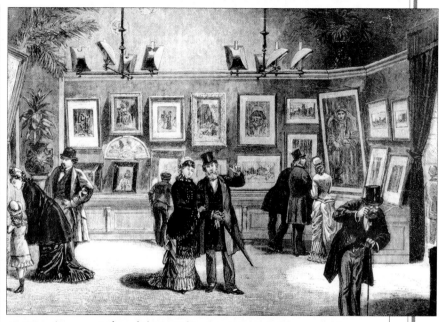

ABOVE: *A room at the exhibition of Impressionist works mounted by Durand-Ruel at the Grafton Galleries in London, winter 1905.*

not always entirely uncritical of Monet, in particular of his lack of 'finish' (which he perceived to be, not incorrectly an occasional obstruction to sales), and the high prices he began to demand, Monet often chose to show with Durand-Ruel only when the majority of the works in the exhibition had already been sold.

Durand-Ruel kept up his international connections, organizing major shows in London and the very influential *Works in Oils and Pastel by the Impressionists of Paris* in New York in 1886. He staged most (though not all) of Monet's later one-man shows, including the *Cathédrales de Rouen* in 1896, the *Bassin aux Nymphéas* pictures in 1900, the *Vues de la Tamise à Londres* in 1904, and *Les Nymphéas: Séries de paysages d'eau* in 1909. When he died in 1922 he was the leading French art dealer.

RIGHT: **The Cliff Walk at Pourville, 1882.** *The small resort of Pourville, to the west of Dieppe, provided welcome artistic stimulus for Monet on his travels. This attractive and airy scene shows cliff walkers admiring the sea view above Dieppe.*

LEFT: **The Manneporte, Etretat, 1883**. *Monet made several painting expeditions to the Normandy coast during the 1880s. He was particularly attracted by the unusual rock formations there.*

than 20,000 francs. This was the end of the real financial difficulties that had intermittently plagued him, and from then on he was free to do more or less what he liked and go where he liked in search of inspiration. In 1883 Durand-Ruel gave Monet an important one-man exhibition, and although the dealer himself had run into financial problems in 1882 with the collapse of the bank that backed him, this does not seem to have inhibited him greatly. Through him Monet established a price level for his works that would only increase from then on.

During the 1880s Monet was restless and frequently on the move. The prime reason was clearly an unending search for new subjects to paint, but his delicate family situation may have had something to do with it. While travelling, he wrote constantly to Alice, always addressing her as 'Chère Madame' and retaining the formal 'vous'. Tenderness is clearly present,

ABOVE: **Etretat: The Needle and the Porte d'Aval, 1882–86.** *This strangely shaped painting was designed to fit into the panel of a wardrobe door in Monet's hotel.*

RIGHT: *Hiroshige's woodblock print of a rocky coast from* Famous Views of Various Provinces, 1853–6. *This print may well have influenced Monet's paintings of the coastal scene. However, these cliffs had been painted by several noted landscapists, most recently by Courbet.*

RIGHT: *A late nineteenth-century photograph of the Manneporte. This distinctive arch, and the ruffled waters around it, produced fascinating light effects which Monet captured in his paintings.*

however: in October 1885, to Alice from Etretat, he wrote, 'Like you, I've had enough of this separation, and worry about the future.'

Monet's first travels at this period were connected with renewing contact with his brother Léon, resident in Rouen. While there he went on a painting expedition to the coast at Petites Dalles, which he probably knew from his childhood. The following year he revisited other scenes of his youth at Fécamp and Trouville. From Fécamp he wrote to Durand-Ruel suggesting a sizeable advance against the eventual purchase of work he intended to do there; the money would enable him to stay on longer and develop certain ideas for pictures he had in mind. In September 1881 he was back on the Normandy coast, at Sainte-Adresse. The following February he wandered along the Normandy coast westwards from Dieppe, complaining bitterly that he could find nowhere that inspired him, until he lighted on the small resort of Pourville. He found his stay there so productive that in June he

brought Alice and the children down for nearly four months, finally returning to Poissy in October. Late in the year he began a commission to decorate the salon in Durand-Ruel's flat, where he worked on and off until 1895. One of the problems of Pourville, apparently, was that it offered insufficient shelter for the winter in bad weather: 'I can't work in all weathers here as I did in Fécamp. There are no shelters, no crannies in the cliff where I can sit up when it is raining.' When he found his way to Etretat the following year he resolved such problems, as often as not, by painting from the windows of the Hôtel Blanquet on the seafront, facing the cliffs of Port d'Amont with their distinctive arch formation. These cliffs had already been painted, by Courbet among others. (Monet remarked on the difficulty of following the older master in this subject, but was confident of his own ability.)

ABOVE: *A sketch by Monet of the cliffs at Etretat, made around 1885. It is one of a series recorded in his notebooks of the period.*

Clearly he enjoyed Etretat, despite a few battles with bad weather when he ventured out of his hotel; in 1885 Guy de Maupassant described (with perhaps some journalistic exaggeration) an occasion when, braving the elements, Monet 'seized with both hands a shower beating relentlessly on the sea and flung it down on canvas'. In general, Etretat provides an excellent example of Monet's ability to assume tunnel vision, disregarding anything not immediately to his purpose. Some of the wildest views of the cliffs were in fact painted from the safe side of the promenade in this popular and populous seaside resort. Although there were probably few trippers present on Monet's first winter visit in 1883, the town must have been packed on his return in August 1884, and still fairly crowded when he went again with Alice and the children in September 1885, to a house borrowed from his friend and patron Faure. At the Hôtel Blanquet, Monet painted, in traditional artist's style, on the walls and furniture of his hotel room. In the Art Gallery of Ontario in Toronto is a painting of the cliff at Etretat on a sunny but evidently slightly choppy day, weirdly shaped to fit the cheap, gilt, rococo frame of a panel in the wardrobe door (see page 91).

Monet's Artistic Technique

IT IS CURIOUS to think that Monet, the ultimate dissolver of form into colour, actually began as a draughtsman. He became a painter more or less by chance, and his earliest known paintings all conform reasonably closely with academic expectations: the subjects are landscape or still life, the colours are mostly dark and laid on solidly. But soon his palette lightened, his forms became simplified, and dappled effects of light began to filter in. Monet's *Déjeuner sur l'herbe* was a conscious attempt to compose a major work. As the title suggests, the influence of Manet, with his paintings of modern life, bulked large at the time.

Ultimately Monet and Manet, so different in attitude and background, were to diverge – though not before Monet had taught Manet the importance of painting in the open air, on the spot. This was to become and remain the basis of Monet's painting, however much he might modify work afterwards in the studio. His major preoccupation was with light, the way in which it passed over and changed forms, and the necessity of capturing the effect of the moment. Rapidly he became aware that this was something rarely possible in literally applied *plein-air* painting, and, even if a painting was completely executed in front of what it represented, still Monet was essentially painting what was in his head rather than the external phenomena that first inspired the work.

The practicalities of painting outside the studio, even if not adhered to rigidly, dictated much in Monet's evolving technique. In the first instance, it required the work to be dashed down quickly, an impression rather than something deeply pondered, analyzed and formalized. Other incidentals were a thinning-down of the amount of paint put on the canvas and a much more glancing, feathery structure of brushstrokes. Also – a matter of the artist's observation affecting technique – Monet noted that light in uncontrolled, non-studio conditions did not always do what it was supposed to do. Shadows, for example, were not necessarily black: they might be shades of blue or puce; the effect might be obtained boldly by using complementary colours, which intellectual logic said could not possibly be there.

From the mature achievement of his Impressionist style, early in the 1870s, the story of Monet's stylistic, and so of his technical, development becomes almost entirely one of closer and closer approaches to abstraction. As he became increasingly obsessed with capturing the most fleeting effects of light, he realized that single paintings of any given subject were likely to lose immediacy by producing a balanced synthesis of many different effects, different moments. The answer was series painting, in which the effects of different times of day or different states of the weather could be explored separately. Thus in Monet's majestic depictions, or evocations, of Rouen Cathedral, for example, no one picture seeks to tell the whole story. Our final idea of the Cathedral is a fusion of many that Monet creates, not on any single canvas, but in the spectator's head.

During his later years at Giverny, Monet concentrated more and more on tiny variations of one motif, until the water-lilies on the pond are almost cut from their moorings in objective reality to become areas of pure colour moving among other areas of other pure colours. In these final paintings, pattern is only very hazily tied to representation. The paint became thinner and flatter, its application looser and looser. Despite, indeed partly because of, problems with his eyesight, Monet's technical innovation continued to evolve and develop until the end of his life.

RIGHT: *This cartoon from the magazine* Le Charivari, *entitled 'Springtime Soup', satirizes Monet's rapid brushstrokes.*

BELOW: *A pencil sketch of cows on a river bank from around 1895–90. Monet's notebook shows his increasing interest in the compositional possibilities of symmetrical reflections.*

RIGHT: **The Signal, Gare St Lazare, 1876.** *The most daringly composed and executed of Monet's Gare St Lazare canvases. Contemporary critics were impressed by both the modernity and the threatening aspects of the artist's subject.*

Between the first and second visits to Etretat Monet was to make another important move. The lease on the house in Poissy ran out in April 1883 and again, with a succession of late payments of rent and general failure to meet bills, Monet had not endeared himself to his landlords. He and Alice began a systematic exploration further down-river from Poissy in search of somewhere suitable. The train took them to the small town of Vernon and thence on a little branch line to the village of Giverny, just the other side of the Seine. The property they looked at, Le Pressoir, was a rambling, unpretentious house set in a large, neglected walled garden. Arrangements were rapidly concluded, and for ten days Monet, Alice and the older children transported packages. The final move, on 24 April, was the occasion of a slight financial mishap. On their arrival at the station, the Monet-Hoschedé family found that they did not have enough money for all to buy tickets: Monet and some of the children went ahead and the following morning, after an urgent appeal to Durand-Ruel, Alice and the others followed.

Monet does not seem at first to have recognized Giverny as more than a convenient bolt-hole. Having settled the family there, he went off in December with Renoir on a pleasure trip to the Riviera. and to visit

BELOW: *A photograph of the East Bay at Mentone around the date of Monet's visit to the Riviera. It shows the dramatic wild hills of the garrique, long since covered with apartment blocks.*

Cézanne in Aix-en-Provence. But for Monet it was also a search for new subjects and above all a new range of tones. In January he returned to the south alone, swearing Durand-Ruel to secrecy:

> I must beg you not to mention this trip to anyone, not because it is my deep dark secret, but because I need to do it alone. Though I greatly enjoyed travelling there with Renoir as a tourist, it would be very difficult for me to work there with him. I have always worked best on my own, entirely from my own impressions. So keep my secret until I tell you otherwise. If he knew I was going, Renoir would surely want to go with me, and that would be a disaster for both of us.

At first he found the light too brilliant for him to paint without a great deal of damping-down to achieve his own kind of colour harmonies. The landscape as a whole seemed too luxuriant: he was really, he announced, more at home with isolated trees and broad spaces. All the same, he became fascinated, and stayed on painting in Bordighera and Mentone until mid-April 1884. He came back to Giverny with at least 45 paintings, which he showed to Durand-Ruel as material for a new one-man show, beginning already to think of paintings as groups on a particular theme. Durand-Ruel selected 21 of them, and Monet continued to work them up in his studio at Giverny for two months before he (and presumably Durand-Ruel) was satisfied with them. He was initially worried, because, as he wrote to Alice:

ABOVE: *A contemporary view of palm trees at Bordighera, now part of Italy's Mediterranean coast.*

> I did a lot of terrible painting at the beginning, but now I've got the hang of this magical landscape, and I'm desperately eager to convey the enchantment of it. Of course people will say it's all unreal and that I'm mad, but too bad. In any case, they say that when I paint our part of the world. All I do has the iridescent colours of flaming brandy or a pigeon's breast, yet even so I am just taking the first timid steps.

Still, life was complicated for him. While he was in Bordighera, Alice had a crisis of conscience and wrote to him dramatically, misinterpreting something he had written to her and suggesting that they should break off their

RIGHT: **Bordighera, 1884.** *Monet relished the effects of colour and light that he perceived in the South: 'After terrible Belle-Ile this is going to be tender, here's nothing but blue, rose and gold'.*

RIGHT: **Antibes seen from the Plateau Notre-Dame, 1888.** *A celebrated example of Monet's favoured motif of the single pine tree.*

affair. He wrote back, calming her and observing wistfully, 'I wish you would be content to love me as I love you, and could contrive to be a little more reasonable about it.' However, his later letters from the trip are full of expressions of affection, and this crisis, like all the others, was smoothed over. Of greater practical significance were Durand-Ruel's financial problems during the year. He was buying an important body of work from Monet but had difficulty meeting the payments, and sometimes required extended delays. May 1884 found Monet in Paris, penniless by his own account, apologizing for bothering Durand-Ruel at such a time. Throughout the year he kept on at Durand-Ruel, moaning, cajoling and indulging in emotional blackmail. At one stage he said that Durand-Ruel was the only one he trusted, which was probably true, and praised his energy and courage. It is, as usual, difficult to work out how urgent were Monet's needs, and how

much came merely from the habit of complaining. Certainly, even after he told Pissarro that Durand-Ruel's determination had carried him over the worst patch, the letters demanding money continued.

During the rest of 1884 and 1885 Monet stayed fairly close to home, content with his visits to Etretat, repeated again early in 1886. In April of that year he was invited by a diplomat in the French embassy to The Hague to spend a few days working in Holland. He painted tulips and windmills, producing five images in 12 days. These were no doubt subsequently worked over and completed, but all the same the Dutch paintings seem rather perfunctory: Monet was never the man to paint on commission if he could avoid it. Such a specific invitation was unlikely to fire his imagination as would a place that he had decided to explore on his own initiative.

His next trip was to the remote Belle-Ile, off the Brittany coast. He arrived there in September 1886, just at the end of the season and in good, sunny weather. He did not take to the place at all, finding it overwhelmingly melancholy and, even in the sunshine, sinister. But when he was just about to leave, the weather changed to violent storms and driving rain, and he suddenly found that the island held, after all, much that inspired him to paint. The stormy scenes he painted on Belle-Ile suggest an astonishing degree of creative excitement: the little, choppy brushstrokes seem to peck at the canvas rather as the rain and spray must have attacked the artist's face.

For his next significant painting trip Monet, following some kind of deep-laid instinct, went to the opposite extreme: after the northern rigours of Belle-Ile, he spent four months of 1888 at Antibes (where he lived with the painter Henri Harpignies) and Juan-les-Pins. Typically, he did not paint any of the then-famous Mediterranean views, but virtually confined himself to his formula of a solitary tree against the sea – epitomised by the painting entitled *Antibes*. Several times he himself expressed mystification

ABOVE: *A coloured woodblock print by Hiroshige from* Famous Views of Various Provinces, *1853–56. Prints from this series undoubtedly influenced Monet's series of stormy seas around the rocks of Belle-Ile painted in the 1880s.*

as to why some feature, perhaps a rock or tree or stretch of water, should set his creative juices flowing, and others, practically indistinguishable, did not do it at all. The random quality of his inspiration was even more tellingly demonstrated in February 1889, when his new friend Gustave Geffroy, whom he had met on Belle-Ile, took him and two other friends to a part of France that Monet did not know, the valley of the Creuse in the Massif Central (see page 7).

Monet was immediately very excited by the rocky terrain, and he returned alone in March for two-and-a-half months' solid painting. This time it was painting of a different kind from anything that had gone before. Although he had sometimes painted essentially the same subject several times, from different angles or in different weathers, it was on this trip to the Creuse Valley that he began for the first time to paint systematically in series, showing the same views (two of them, one up-river, one down-river, from the same viewpoint at different times of day, and consequently with completely different colour values. It was a discovery he was to work on and elaborate for the rest of his life.

There is no missing the violent surge of artistic excitement that overwhelmed Monet as he reacted to the landscape and realized its possibilities. These paintings are strongly, even stridently, coloured: an acid blue in the clouds set against a brilliant orange sunset sky, or frosty blues and purples in the distant hillside against a bilious green-brown in the foreground rocks, so as almost to set the teeth on edge. These are not careful paintings, considerate of their audience. Monet had always been confident and determined to go his own way, especially after he had abandoned in the late 1870s any hopes he might have nurtured for success in the Salon. But never had he been so confident, never so sure that, whatever critics and buyers might say, what he was doing here was right for him, the only way he could go. Everything about the pictures proclaims that, on the verge of his half century, Monet had been granted a new lease of life.

GIVERNY: THE SERIES PAINTINGS

IN 1890 MONET FOUND THAT he had enough money to buy outright the house he and his heterodox family had been living in for the past seven years. In March the following year Ernest Hoschedé, long since effectively vanished from his family's life, died. After a decent interval, in July 1892 Monet and Alice were quietly married in Giverny, with Monet's brother Léon and the faithful Caillebotte among the witnesses. This must have been a great relief for Alice, who was religiously devout and so had nothing of the bohemian in her background, and so had been disturbed by the irregular nature of her relationship with Monet ever since they first openly challenged convention by moving together to Poissy in 1880.

There seems no doubt that the oddity of Monet's situation with the Hoschedés had been a factor in his progressive withdrawal from the friends of his youth, the other Impressionists and the art world of Paris in general. His earlier life with Camille had not been exceptional in his circle. Several of the other Impressionists, including Manet, Pissarro and Renoir, did as Monet: they became involved with their favourite models and fathered illegitimate children eventually setting the record straight by marrying their mistresses and legitimizing the children. But Monet's involvement with Alice Hoschedé was different, and definitely more scandalous, in that she was a respectably married woman of good family, and he himself a widower and father of two sons.

Part, at least, of Monet's progressive isolation probably came about because he wished it so. He was not at heart convivial and needed to be alone for much of the time in order to work effectively: although in the early days he had joined happily in communal painting expeditions – with Renoir especially, but also on occasion with Sisley, Manet and Pissarro –

later on he could not accept the company of even Renoir, except purely socially. What he needed in life was what he finally got: ample time to work on his own, interspersed with interludes of secure life as part of a family, which he happily dominated, loved and looked after – the perfect patriarch. A domain, to shape and control, was an important part of this. How else could he ensure that he was truly at the centre of a private world?

This was reflected in the deep but narrow focus of his paintings in this period, which worked repeatedly over the same small group of subjects to explore relentlessly their formal possibilities. Almost all of his subjects during the 1890s, up until 1899, were found in the immediate vicinity of Giverny. Apart from a single trip to Norway, he went no further afield than Rouen, only 70 kilometres from Giverny as the crow flies (nearer, in fact, than Paris) and familiar as the home of his brother Léon, with a couple of interludes on the nearby Normandy coast.

Monet's first deliberate attempt to practice series painting took place in the Creuse Valley in 1889. He had been tending in this direction for some years, however painting loose groups of canvases in concentrated bouts in a particular place, so that the same motifs naturally recur, in various combinations, and seen from various angles. This was quite common among painters in France at the time, particularly landscape painters, who often in the autumn exhibited what they had done with their summer. But Monet was developing a much more systematic idea. Although retaining a reputation as the least intellectual of painters (in accordance with Cézanne's early judgment of him: 'Only an eye – but what an eye!'), it is unmistakable that a great deal of thought and planning was going into the series paintings of the 1890s. Monet knew exactly what he was doing in them, though he may have been reticent in admitting it, even to intimates and such professionals as Durand-Ruel. An

ABOVE: *The extended family at Giverny in the 1880s. From left to right: Monet, Alice, Michel Monet (seated on the ground), Jean-Pierre seated beside Alice, Blanche, Jean Monet, Jacques (standing) and the three Hoschedé daughters, Marthe, Germaine, and Suzanne.*

unusually explicit account by Monet of what he had in mind at the very beginning of this period does exist, however. He wrote frequently to his friend (and eventual biographer) Geffroy, often complaining. On 25 July 1890, for instance, he wrote:

> I am in a very bad mood and deeply disgusted with the very idea of painting. It really is a continuous torture. Don't expect to see anything new. I have been able to do very little, and what I have done is destroyed, scraped down or torn up. You can't imagine what abominable weather we've had unendingly these last two months. When you're trying to evoke the weather, the atmosphere, and the general feeling of things, it's enough to drive you out of your mind with sheer fury. In addition to all this, I've been stupid enough to get a bout of rheumatism. I'm paying for my sessions in rain and snow; it's depressing to think I shall have to give up painting in all weathers, and work out of doors only when it's fine. Life really is stupid.

But by 7 October all had changed. Black moods forgotten, Monet wrote to Geffroy that he was concentrating on pictures of *meules* (grainstacks, not necessarily of hay):

> I'm slaving away, working determinedly on a series of effects, but at this time of year the sun goes down so fast I can't keep up with it. I am becoming so slow in my work it makes me desperate, but the further I get the more clearly I realize how much I have to work in order to capture what I am looking for: 'instantaneity', above all, the same enveloping light spread over everything. More than ever simple things arrived at all in one go disgust me. Finally, I am more and more enflamed by the need to render exactly what I experience, and I vow to live on productively because it seems to me that I shall continue to progress. You see that I am in a good mood...

The key to this, and to the series paintings as a whole, is the speed at which the light changes. Painting in the south, Monet had appreciated the long hot days of uniform, almost imperceptibly changing, light, which gave him

ABOVE: *A lane into the village of Giverny at about the time Monet settled there. In later years the French state decreed the building of a tarmac road for the convenience of Monet's stream of distinguished visitors.*

RIGHT: **Grainstacks: End of Summer: Morning Effect, 1891.** *Monet selected the motif of grainstacks for his first deliberate attempt to create a 'series' of paintings, the value of which would lie in their relationship to one another.*

RIGHT: **Grainstacks: End of Summer: Evening Effect, 1891.** *The subject of grainstacks held symbolic value for the French at this period, signifying peace and plenty. However, there were practical problems for the artist to deal with, as the peasants delighted in moving them whilst he painted.*

time enough to capture its effects. In the north, things were very different: a particular effect of light seldom persisted for more than ten minutes at the most. Monet had either to paint very fast indeed, or to return to the subject at exactly the same moment each day for a long as he could before the cycle of the seasons too markedly changed the quality of the light. Monet was certainly capable, when necessary, of painting very quickly indeed, but he did not like doing so and, as he remarked to Geffroy, he became increasingly sceptical about the value of such unconsidered chance effects.

He had always had problems with capturing the transitory effect. In 1886 he had written to Alice from Belle-Ile:

The weather was good today, and I worked hard, though perhaps not well. It's getting harder and harder because I want to finish, and to do that I have to find exactly the same effect again each day, which of course often does not work out, as the sun changes course from day to day, and the light does not fall in the same way. In any case, the weather varies so much that I would need to go out with all my canvases in a cart; I often

select what I am to take according to the weather, and then find I can't work on them because, as with today, the weather changes on my way to the location. You can imagine what kind of mood I'm in after that, but since I know things have to be brought to some conclusion, I pretty well have to transform some paintings completely.

An answer, therefore, was to paint in series, having several canvases of the same subject from the same viewpoint on the go at the same time, so that he could replace one with another as the light shifted in angle and changed in quality. Although he had investigated this approach to a limited degree in the Creuse Valley, and subsequently extended it in paintings of the poppyfields around Giverny, he evidently felt that there was an exciting new element in his pictures of the grainstacks.

The series seems to have begun from a chance observations one day when Monet went with his stepdaughter (probably Blanche, who was already showing an interest in painting) to make a study of a particular stack in the field next door to his house and was struck by the wonderful effects of the constantly changing light. He suddenly conceived the idea of making a whole series of momentary observations that would, as he told a journalist in 1891, 'acquire their value only by comparison and succession over the entire series'. It has been possible to work out from contemporary photographs that

BELOW: *A photograph of grainstacks seen from Monet's studio, published in the magazine* L'Art et les Artistes, *1905.*

the location of the stacks was the Clos Morin, just to the west of Monet's property in Giverny, and that he probably did not have to go any further to paint them than the boundary of his garden. Having begun to paint them in October, he continued to work on them throughout the winter, hence the fact that some of them are snow scenes. Monet intermittently kept Durand-Ruel informed of what he was doing, apologizing for neglecting his correspondence and giving as his reason the fact that he was working outdoors all day. He already knew how he wanted the *Grainstacks* to be exhibited, but kept silent about it until he had a range of pictures to show Durand-Ruel. He quietly discouraged the dealer from staging another group show of the Impressionists (Monet had not taken part in the eighth and last exhibition in 1886), suggesting it made more sense to keep to one-man shows.

When Durand-Ruel did see a significant number of the grainstack pictures together, he immediately recognized that they represented a new and important development in Monet's work, and he set aside a special section of the show of *Oeuvres récentes de Cl. Monet* in May 1891 to show 15 of them together. The result was quite sensational: Monet's universal acceptance as one of the masters of French art can be dated from this time, although inevitably there were still some stragglers complaining about his paintings' lack of 'finish'. In a way Monet encouraged this himself, by sticking to accounts of his working methods that minimized or denied altogether the role of the studio, or of second thoughts and retouching after the first fine frenzy of creation. It was exactly this spontaneous approach that Monet had expounded in the magazine *La Vie Moderne*, and which he continued to maintain into old age. His intimates, of course, knew otherwise: with Durand-Ruel, for instance, he was always frank about his need of time for reconsideration. In November 1886, in answer to Durand-Ruel's urgent requests for whatever he had finished on Belle-Ile, he wrote testily:

ABOVE: *A sketch of the grainstacks from Monet's notebook of drawings between 1888 and 1891, showing how he eliminated all traces of human presence to concentrate on the placing of the motif.*

LEFT: **Poplars in Sunlight, 1891.** *The poplar, winding along the banks of the nearby River Epte and long a symbol of France, provided Monet's next motif. However, the artist was again forced to pay off the wily locals who threatened to chop down the ranks of trees.*

RIGHT: **Poplars Series: Effect of Wind, 1891.** *The poplars motif offered Monet the chance to explore the effects of light on a moving subject, in contrast to the solidity of the grainstacks. This resulted in the most dramatic and inventively decorative of the series paintings.*

Nothing is finished, and you know perfectly well that I really can't judge what I've done until I get home with the pictures and have a chance to look over them again. I always need a short interval before I can put the finishing touches to them. I'm still hard at work, and unfortunately with the continuing bad weather it is very difficult to find again the effects I want for many of my subjects, so I shall have a lot to do when I get home to Giverny.

In response to similar urgings from Durand-Ruel when he returned from Bordighera and Mentone in 1884, he had said firmly:

I don't have a single canvas that does not need to be looked at again and carefully retouched, and that cannot be done in a day. I need to look over all my work relaxedly, and in the proper conditions. I have been working for three months face to face with nature, going to a lot of trouble and never being totally satisfied. It's really only here in the last few days that I see what needs to be done with some of the pictures. You have to understand that out of the numerous studies I have made, not all can be put on the market. Some could be excellent, I think, and others, though a bit lacking in definition, might turn out very well if they are carefully retouched. But, I repeat, this cannot be done from one day to the next.

From his private correspondence it is evident that, even with works painted as close to home as the *Grainstacks*, the period of reflection and retouching was still necessary to him. Writing to Durand-Ruel's son Charles in June

1891, he said that he would have the six pictures Durand-Ruel had bought on his last visit delivered the following day, but added, 'Two of them still need some finishing touches. They are the two of the grainstacks. You can hold on to the other four, and please sent these two back in the same crate.' In fact, it was only to be expected that more reworking would be necessary if the pictures were to be considered not one by one, as separate entities, but as part of a larger whole. If the series was to be shown together, adjustments would be needed to produce a satisfying overall balance of effect.

Monet's physical methods of working at this time are not altogether clear. The statesman George Clemenceau, who was a friend of the artist, subsequently published a recollection of Monet painting the poppyfields near Giverny that he worked on immediately before embarking on the grainstacks series. According to Clemenceau, Monet on that occasion had four easels set up side by side, and moved backwards and forwards from one painting to another with great speed, capturing each little variation of light as it passed over. One of Monet's stepsons firmly denied that he ever painted with more than one easel, there being no more than one ideal viewpoint, and that he simply worked through the nearby pile of pictures in progress one by one as the hands moved round the clock. This is probably true of the next series Monet was to undertake, of Rouen Cathedral, but it is by no means certain that he did not sometimes experiment with different lines of approach to the same central problem. There are reliable records, later on, of his having several easels set up at different points in his water garden, so that he could work at any time on any of several different pictures in hand simultaneously.

The idea of Monet's returning to the town for the Rouen Cathedral paintings is on the face of it rather surprising. The process of turning his back on the urban scene seemed to have been complete with his purchase of the property in Giverny. In fact, painting in Rouen at all, let alone painting an extended series, was no part of Monet's plans. His presence in

ABOVE: **Nizamu, Yellow Dusk, c. 1845–55**: *A woodblock print from Hiroshige's series* Fifty-three Stations of the Tokaido. *The Japanese artist's successful exploitation of decorative possibilities in these slender and elegant trees would not be lost on Monet.*

Rouen, it emerges, was required for purely business reasons: his half-sister Marie had just died suddenly, and Monet and his brother Léon had to settle her estate. Marie was the child of Monet's father and his father's former mistress, a maid in the household, whom he had married only in 1870, a few months before his death. The father's estate, which included some important early paintings by Monet, had been divided among the three children, and Monet and his brother now wanted to acquire the paintings that had fallen to Marie's share. They were able to do so at a reasonable price from Marie's mother, who survived Marie. Léon afterwards invited Monet to return with him to Rouen, which Monet agreed to do, though he did not want the distraction of staying with Léon and instead booked himself into a hotel, just near the cathedral. He started work at once on two panoramic views of the town, neither of which he was to finish.

Disgruntled, he wrote home to Alice, 'I really can't stand living in towns, and I'm very fed up, especially since nothing here is going the way I want.' He added that he could not wait to be home the following day. But some kind of seed had been sown in his mind. In the same letter he spoke with guarded optimism of having after all perhaps found a subject, and how, in pursuit of that, he had been able to take over an unoccupied apartment right opposite the cathedral. He had in fact already painted two views of the cathedral's north-west tower, from street level, but, with the discovery of the first-floor apartment, he had hit upon his real subject, the west façade. Before he got back to Giverny he had at least roughed out the first two paintings in the main body of work that was to prove one of his most famous series.

In these first two pictures Monet tackled the façade absolutely straight-on, with the subject almost symmetrically disposed on the canvas. If, as seems likely, he went home to Giverny on 13 February, he was delayed there by ill health, as well as by the necessity of going to Paris to assist

ABOVE: *A ninteenth-century photograph of the West Façade of Rouen Cathedral. The tall spire in the background was eliminated from Monet's motif.*

LEFT: **Portail St Romain, Rouen Cathedral: Morning Effect, 1894.** *Monet worked in cramped quarters in a shopfront in the main square surrounded by his stacked canvases. He worked on these in rotation as the light changed, unable to step back and observe his progress.*

RIGHT: **Rouen Cathedral, West Façade: Sunlight, 1894**. *Another of the Rouen Cathedral paintings showing the strong light effect of midday. Monet was fortunate in having consistently good weather during his visits to Rouen.*

Durand-Ruel with the hanging of his next show, devoted to paintings of the poplars around Giverny. He did not get back to Rouen until 25 February, by which time the apartment was occupied by workers laying a new floor. However, he was able to find alternative accommodation in a neighbouring property, slightly to the south of the first, and was further mollified by the excellent weather. In all, he painted the cathedral from three different first-floor properties across the cathedral square during the three months, February to April, that he spent in Rouen during 1892 and again in 1893, from February to April. All three locations were so close together that it is not easy to distinguish which of the 28 canvases were painted from which building, though it is reasonable to suppose that the most unequivocally frontal images are from the first and the most sharply angled from the third. On the other hand, he was perfectly capable of rearranging physical facts to suit his aesthetic purposes (by eliminating, for instance, all evidence of the cathedral's Neo-Gothic central spire after the first two paintings), and he could well have 'cropped' his compositions in different ways even if working always from the same viewpoint.

This is not to mention the unusual amount of balancing and retouching, if not total reworking, the series underwent in Giverny, when Monet had finished at Rouen. We know that he early on saw the pictures of the cathedral as a series, and a very tightly plotted one at that. In March a local collector in Rouen, François Depeaux, was trying hard to persuade Monet to sell him two of the paintings immediately, one for himself, the other for the local museum. Monet was determined to do no such thing, as he felt he had to finish the whole series, however many that might eventually be, see them all together in Giverny and finish them to his own satisfaction before he would consider showing

Monet's Family of Painters

As MONET'S FAME GREW, he began to attract disciples around him in Giverny. Although he never had any pupils, he was inclined to be friendly and forthcoming towards other painters in the locality, particularly the group of young Americans who began to assemble there in 1887. Two American artists, Willard Metcalf and Theodore Robinson, had visited Monet in 1885, but they did not start to live and work in Giverny until the summer of 1887, when they arrived with five others: Theodore Wendel (who had painted there the previous year), Louis Ritter, Henry Fitch Taylor, John Leslie Breck and the Canadian William Blair Bruce, as well as Breck's mother and brother. Visitors in such numbers persuaded the owners of the local café, Lucien and Angelina Baudy, to open a hotel-cum-studio for artists.

Monet seemed to welcome some of them, particularly Robinson and Breck, into his family circle. His own painting had considerable influence on Robinson, who was to become a leading American Impressionist, but the whole group was reverential and tributes to Monet abounded, notably the series of *12 Studies of an Autumn Day* painted by Breck in 1891, pictures of grainstacks at various hours of the day clearly inspired by the series of grainstack pictures painted by Monet during the previous year. Unfortunately, at some stage, probably in 1891, Breck showed signs of becoming romantically involved with Alice Hoschedé's second daughter Blanche, who was then aged about 25.

Blanche was the only one among Monet's numerous children and stepchildren who had shown any sign of artistic talent, and by 1886 his letters show that he had begun to take her ambitions seriously. It is not clear exactly what Monet had against Breck as a suitor for Blanche. He himself suggested that it was simply because he was American and an artist too poor to support a wife. There was probably also an element of quasi-parental jealousy in that Monet always tended to object to anything that might break up his little clan and no doubt resented the way that the affair had gone on in secret.

Once Breck had been sent packing, Blanche seems to have settled back into the routine of accompanying Monet on his local painting trips and painting on her own behalf. But with three attractive women in his family and a group of lively young American artists in the area, Monet was very soon to encounter more trouble of the same sort. It emerged that Blanche's younger sister Suzanne was being courted by another of the Americans, Theodore Earl Butler, who had arrived in Giverny in 1888. Monet insisted that if Alice could do

LEFT: *A group of family and friends on the terrace at Giverny in 1900 to celebrate the marriage of Marthe Hoschedé and Theodore Earl Butler. Guests included Paul Durand-Ruel (left) and the two sons of Sisley (the artist himself had died the previous year). Monet had just forbidden the marriage of Pierre Sisley and Germaine Hoschedé.*

nothing to break up this romance, he would find it impossible to stay in Giverny any longer and would sell the house. He knew, he added, that Alice always accused him of seeing evil in everything, but everything he had done was because he loved the children. Despite this unpromising beginning, Butler seems to have been able to account for himself satisfactorily. The irate letter was written on 10 March 1892, and on 20 July Butler and Suzanne were married with Monet's blessing – an occasion commemorated in Robinson's painting *The Wedding March*.

In 1897 Blanche, who had continued to live at home, married Monet's elder son Jean – not without some slight misgivings on Monet's part – and the couple moved away, though only as far as Rouen, where Jean worked for his uncle Léon and Blanche painted obsessively, taking part in the Salon des Artistes Indépendants in Paris from 1905 and the Salon des Artiste Rouennais from its inception in 1907. In 1899 Suzanne died, and it fell to the eldest sister, Marthe, to look after the children. In 1900 she became Butler's second wife, so that he and his children remained close to the Monet household, with occasional visits to the United States. In 1911 Alice Monet died, and the following year Jean Monet, taken seriously ill, was moved back to Giverny with Blanche.

After Jean's death in 1914 Blanche went back to live at the family home and gave up painting completely in order to keep house for Monet. She remained faithful in this resolve until his death in 1926, and indeed stayed on in charge of the house in Giverny until 1940, when the house and studio suffered some minor damage during the German invasion. After a brief absence, she returned and stayed in Giverny until her death in 1947, at the age of 82.

Even today the family tradition continues at Giverny. One of Alice Monet's great-grand-children, Jean-Marie Toulgouat, still lives and works there, painting the poppies and poplars of the area in a style which his step-great-grandfather might well recognize and approve.

BELOW: *Germaine Hoschedé and Alice Butler by the lily-pond in 1900 with Monet (right) and Georges Durand-Ruel.*

or selling any of them. Although the weather remained in the main excellent, Monet always feared it would take a turn for the worse. Then there were family troubles at home. They concerned neither of his own sons, who were now respectively 25 and 14, but Suzanne, Alice's daughter. Suzanne had announced that she wanted to marry the 30-year old American painter Theodore Butler, one of a group of American artists who formed a kind of informal artists' colony in the vicinity. Monet raged at Alice by letter:

> It is your duty to prevent your daughter from marrying an American, unless we have become acquainted with him in a respectable way, by a personal contact or formal introduction. Certainly he cannot be someone just met in the street.

Monet may have reacted so violently because he felt possessive about Suzanne, who had probably been his favourite, and certainly his favourite model, among Alice's children. However, Monet soon gave the engagement his blessing and the couple were married in Giverny on 20 July.

After the summer of 1892, Monet seems to have been relatively inactive, perhaps working over the first group of Rouen Cathedral paintings. He was evasive about these with Durand-Ruel, reasserting his determination not to show any until the series was completed and claiming to be frightened by his own 'laziness'. He needed to do more work on the spot in Rouen, and by February 1893 he was back. Again he stayed till mid-April, no doubt still working on the paintings of the previous year as well as initiating some new ones. He wrote constantly to Alice, alternating confidence with complaints, the latter particularly about the weather – even though on grey days he was able to work on his grey-toned paintings (he was, after all, working indoors) and on sunny days could turn to the brighter pictures of the series. And at least he had no complaints about his chosen subject: if he stayed in Rouen for all eternity, he said, he would still see something new every day. But although he toyed with the idea of returning again in 1894, he had really decided to finish the series if he possibly could in 1893. By the time April came, he was dazed with the concentrated effort and felt no longer capable of telling whether he was improving the pictures or not.

RIGHT: **Rouen Cathedral, West Façade, 1894.**
A further subtle shift in the colours observed by Monet as the sunlight moved across the intricately carved façade.

Back in Giverny, he began the formidable task of pulling all the paintings together. Beset by fears of failure, he pecked at them through the summer and the following winter, not satisfied that they were finished until well into 1894, when he signed and dated 26 of the 30. (Three others were signed but not dated, and a fourth was neither signed nor dated, being presumably regarded as unfinished.) He even went on worrying away at them into 1895, since we know from an account of meeting him by the painter-prince Eugen of Sweden that Monet took at least one of them with him to Norway, still dissatisfied with it. They were not actually exhibited until May 1895, when Durand-Ruel included 20 of them in his big Monet show, leaving out all the 'gold-and-red' pictures of the façade in resplendent evening light. This was probably because Monet wanted to avoid all the sentimental and anecdotal connotations of a dawn-to-dusk cycle, insisting instead on a categorization by dominant tonality. The reception of the show, and the *Cathedrals* in particular, was never less than respectful; there was some feeling that those who liked the series paintings least sensed an almost sinful self-indulgence about their gorgeous colouring (one critic called it 'tropical'). Those who liked them most, however, seemed stumped for words that would express precisely what they saw in them.

ABOVE: *A late nineteenth-century photograph of the River Epte near Giverny, bordered by willows and poplars.*

The cathedral paintings are about nothing except the paint itself. There is something telepathic about the way Monet transmitted directly the emotion he felt, close often to ecstasy, as he saw the light, warm or cool, straight-on or slanting, move across the more or less illegible shapes of the carved and cavernous façade. Some of the series may be more 'finished' than others, but none of them moves from the ideal of being an impression rather than a depiction (see page 64). In working these paintings Monet took apart what he saw, and then gradually selected, rearranged and reconstituted it into his own abstract ideal.

In the long months that he was fidgeting over the *Cathedrals,* between April 1893 and May 1895, Monet was by no means inactive in other directions. For one thing, he had already begun to plot the commercial strategy of the *Cathedrals'* marketing. Despite his assertions that he would not sell any before the whole series was complete, he wanted, as usual in the previous few years, to make sure that as many as possible of the pictures in the new show were already sold before it opened – especially since he had already decided early in 1894 that he wanted the unprecedented sum of 15,000 francs for each. Durand-Ruel had the gravest doubts about this, and Monet relented to the extent of agreeing that only the key works of the series need attain that figure. But by September 1894 he was able to tell Durand-Ruel that several of the *Cathedrals* had been sold, even at the highest price, to private collectors. This meant that Durand-Ruel's refusal to buy any of them himself was rendered unimportant.

To provide a setting for the Rouen pictures, which Monet felt strongly should not be exhibited by themselves, he also worked on a variety of themes that he found in the locality of Giverny. Early in 1894 he was out painting a group of pictures centred on the church in nearby Vernon, with the Seine in the foreground. They are glittering evocations of the cool, clear air of winter. As summer approached, he painted a further quartet of pictures, among his most luscious and unashamedly sensuous, of flowering spring meadows with two slim saplings silhouetted against the pale sunny sky. In November his old friend Cézanne came to Giverny on a visit, and Monet, with an unusual burst of sociability, brought him together with his other, more recent friends, Clemenceau, Geffroy and Auguste Rodin.

The following January he was off to Norway. His stepson Jacques was working in Christiania (now known as Oslo) as a shipbuilder. Monet experienced extreme fluctuations of feeling about the country, not liking it at first, then finding it fascinating, then regretting he had come at all. But then Jacques took him to Sandviken, less than an hour away from

ABOVE: Monet Painting in the Flowers at Giverny, 1917. *This sketch by Camille Pissarro's son Manzana, who grew up within the Impressionist group, captures the passion, energy and determination of the now ageing Monet.*

Christiania, and there he discovered a motif to his taste, Mount Kolsaas. By the time he returned to Giverny in April, he had worked on 26 canvases, though at least nine of them were unfinished. Half of the 26 were a virtually uniform series of Mount Kolsaas, all from the same angle and of much the same size; all of them were included in the May exhibition, though only six were signed, usually Monet's way of signifying that he thought the work complete. None of the Norwegian pictures sold, and they were all still in Monet's studio when he died. In this respect, no doubt, they were the least successful commercially of all Monet's series paintings, though in their bold simplicity they impress today as being among Monet's most modern and forward-looking achievements, almost oriental in their sparseness and economy.

One reason for Monet's visit to Norway and inclusion of these canvases in his exhibition (along with one of his 1886 tulip pictures from Holland) may have been that he saw the desirability of appearing before the public as an international figure rather than merely a specialist in painting provincial France. If so, it might explain why London was the subject of his next major series. Before he started that, however, he went back, from February to April in both 1896 and 1897, to his old familiar Normandy stamping grounds of Pourville and Varengeville to produce groups of rather abstracted cliff-top scenes. At home in Giverny he painted another series of misty mornings on the Seine, exhibited together by Georges Petit in June 1898.

Monet had been in London before (see page 51) and had painted there during his self-imposed exile. He had friends and associates in England, among them the painters James McNeill Whistler and John Singer Sargent.

ABOVE: *A contemporary photograph of the Gorge des Moustiers showing elements of the scene excluded by Monet in his paintings.*

RIGHT: **House of the Customs Officer, Varengeville, 1897.**
This cabin on the rocky cliffs above Dieppe had a special significance for Monet. He rearranged the scene in many canvases of the cliffs and gorge, so that the lone cabin facing the sea becomes the only evidence of man.

Photography and Art

WHEN IN 1905 Durand-Ruel reported to Monet that William Rothenstein thought his Rouen Cathedral paintings looked as if they were done from a photograph, and an American artist called Alexander Harrison alleged that Monet had requested from him photographs of London bridges and the Houses of Parliament so that he could finish his London paintings, Monet was dismissive. He said the painter Sargent had asked Harrison to make him a photograph of Parliament, but that he had never been able to use it. It is not easy to see why Rothenstein should think that the Cathedral pictures looked as if they were painted from a photograph; it is hard to imagine paintings with which a small black-and-white photograph could have been of less help.

In Monet's time there was already a strong tradition of using photographs in painting, and on the photography side a passion for 'pictorialism', which usually meant manipulating photographs to make them look as much like paintings as possible. There is some evidence that Ingres, the arch-conservative academic in France, used photographs in his later paintings, and his great rival Delacroix certainly did, having many photographs of nude models specially taken for his use by his friend Eugène Durieux in the 1850s. As the century wore on, more and more photographic albums and collections of photographs appeared, taken and marketed specifically as artists' aids. They were primarily of two kinds. First, there were the photographs of posed models, usually nude, substituting for life classes or hired models. Second, there were collections of photographs of exotic locations and peoples, North Africa and the Middle East being particularly favoured. These, obviously, were meant for the painter who wanted to leap on to the bandwagon of Orientalism, immensely popular throughout most of the nineteenth century because of its exotic biblical overtones and the discreet eroticism it was felt to license.

The usual subject-matter of the Impressionists, and even more their manner of approach to it, meant that photographs were of little use to them. Monet was not worried in principle over the allegation that he made use of photographs; what concerned him slightly was the suggestion it contained that the essential work of his paintings was done in a studio instead of on the spot.

Ironically, the Impressionists owed their first real chance to make a concerted impact, the independent show mounted in 1874, to their friend Félix Tournachon – now better known as a photographer under his professional pseudonym Nadar. Success required him to move to new premises, and having just vacated his old rooms, he lent them to the artists for their first independent show. Thus the first Impressionist exhibition actually took place in a photographer's studio.

LEFT: *A publicity self-portrait of the illustrator and photographer Nadar in his famous balloon from which he took aerial views of the new Paris.*

RIGHT: *Nadar's studio in Paris, where the first Impressionist exhibition was held.*

Over the years he had paid several visits to take part in art exhibitions, or in 1898 to visit his younger son Michel, by then aged 20 and learning English. 'I so love London!' he was to say to the art dealer René Gimpel in 1920,

> but I love it only in winter. It's nice in summer with its parks, but nothing like it is in winter with the fog, for without the fog London wouldn't be a beautiful city. It's the fog that gives it its magnificent breadth. Those massive, regular blocks become grandiose within that mysterious cloak.

When he went to London in September 1899, he went there, travelling specifically to paint, travelling in considerable style with Alice and his youngest stepdaughter Germaine and staying at the fashionable and expensive Savoy Hotel. The plans for this particular episode in Monet's painting career were carefully laid, unlike those for the Rouen Cathedral pictures. With a typical taste for obfuscation, Monet subsequently let it be said that the London pictures were also initiated by chance, on a spontaneous impulse. In 1904 he told an interviewer that, when he came to London to see Michel, he happened to stay in the Savoy, happened to notice the effects of fog from his window overlooking the Thames and was immediately struck with the impulse to paint them, staying on a month to do so. In fact, when he visited Michel in 1898 he did no artistic work and stayed not at the Savoy but at the Grosvenor Hotel. It was probably on that occasion, however, that his plans for painting a series of works in London began to develop.

One of the reasons for concealing the truth may have been that his programme for the London pictures was significantly different from that for the Rouen pictures, throwing into doubt his claim always to paint on the spot, from direct inspiration and observation. In Rouen he seems at least to have begun with the idea of capturing the effects of light at different times of day, which could be repeated (over a limited period) virtually every day, so that all he had to do was to shift his attention from one to another of the

ABOVE: *A review by Geffroy of Monet's major one-man exhibition in 1898 at the Galerie Georges Petit. Monet showed 61 canvases including 18 Mornings on the Seine. The days of his great fame were beginning.*

London in the 1890s

Throughout the second half of the nineteenth century there was tremendous, if largely unspoken, rivalry between London and Paris. Not, perhaps, that Londoners were so conscious of it: they automatically assumed that London was the centre of the world. (Of course, Paris might have the advantage in more frivolous aspects of life: an attractive place to visit, but not to live.) In France, on the other hand, intense patriotism was tied up in the idea that Paris was, or should be, the leading city of the world. To achieve this was one of Napoleon III's principal aims and the cause of Haussmann's re-ordering of the narrow medieval streets into great open avenues and boulevards. It was what the Expositions Universelles were all about.

When Monet visited London for the first time in 1870 he was under some duress as a self-exile, and it was hardly to be expected that he would particularly like the city he saw. He could not have been living in very comfortable circumstances and was possibly staying as far out as his friend Pissarro, who had settled for the duration in Norwood. Most of the bustle, the glamour, the luxury of London at that point must have passed him by. He painted in the London parks and on the Embankment near Charing Cross. Almost all we know of his attitudes we know from the few paintings accomplished during his exile, which seem to express gloom, detachment and perhaps a certain dawning appreciation of London as a city of mists and mystery.

When Monet came back to paint in 1899 things were standing very differently, both with London and with him. By now he could afford to travel in luxury and to stay in the new Savoy Hotel. Open for little more than a decade, it was regarded as one of the most luxurious hotels in the world, 'overlooking,' to quote a brochure of 1900, 'the River Thames and the Embankment Gardens. By day the most beautiful garden and river view in Europe: by night a fairy scene.' A suite on the river front such as Monet enjoyed cost upwards of 30 shillings a night, a considerable sum at the time. London, too, had changed. Now reaching the zenith of its imperial

ABOVE: *An article in the* Illustrated London News *of 1900 on the newly built Savoy Hotel, London, included a full-page set of engravings detailing its luxuries.*

splendour, it was a Mecca for tourists, including many French who came, improbably, for the food: the unrivalled roast meats, the rich and filling puddings and the drinks specially cultivated in England, such as whisky, port and sherry, and those exotic English beers.

RIGHT: **London, the Parliament: a Ray of Sunshine Through Fog, 1904.** *Monet delighted in the dramatic visual effects produced by the famous London fogs.*

In his *Londres comme je l'ai vu*, published in 1908 (hot on the heels of *Berlin comme je l'ai vu* and *New York comme je l'ai vu*), the illustrator and writer Charles Huard meditated on the strange fascination of London in the 1900s, around the time Monet was regularly there. Inevitably he started with the weather.

> I have known Frenchmen who, unable to bear it, went straight back to their house, buckled their bags and got on the train again with the feeling that they had been living for some hours in a nightmare country.

However, he himself rhapsodized over the Thames, with its magical mists, and the hallucinatory quality of London nights. He found plenty of picturesque buildings to see, venturing as far out as Kew. And he really liked the food, inviting French gourmets to sample the delights of the city inns as well as observing the distinctive British brand of barmaid, who, he alleged, 'delight in romantic Christian names and are likely to be called Elizabeth, Margaret, Margorie (sic) or Gladys like the heroines of the tuppenny novels designed for their reading.'

One suspects that little of this had any effect on Monet, though he had friends and acquaintances in London and ate out on occasion. For him it was above all the weather that furnished the interest and the raw material for art. At the time there was little concern for the ecological implications of all the coal dust in the air, but even the least sensitive saw that the constant smog and the pall of soot over everything, far worse than in Paris, had its sinister side as well as its rather hellish beauty. Many poets and writers had noticed these patterns of light and shade, but the foreign artist, looking with an outsider's eyes, was particularly fascinated by them. However, he was to find the shifting weather conditions problematic and on occasions feared the changes would completely ruin the painting. In March 1900 Monet wrote home:

> This morning I thought the weather had changed completely when I got up I was horrified to find there was no fog, not even the faintest trace of a fog....But then, little by little, the fires were lit, and the smoke and fog came back.

several paintings in hand as the day progressed. Naturally this proved too neat a scheme to work in practice, as many of the effects that most struck him existed for only a few moments and never returned at all. In effect, he painted more from what existed in his head than from the actuality in front of him, evoking the impression of instantaneity through long sessions of retouching in the studio. An unwilling recognition of this seems to have been built into the London painting sessions from the start and, although he showed Durand-Ruel the canvases he brought back from London in November 1899 and Durand-Ruel selected 11 of them, he temporized about when he would finish them and kept putting off the finalization of his London works. By then he knew that, even if his vision as a painter had to be inspired by momentary experiences, their realization in paint demanded a long, slow process. Notations of these fleeting perceptions had to be brought into line with Monet's elusive artistic ideal.

RIGHT: A photograph of the Thames in about 1900, showing the new Savoy Hotel (centre right) from which Monet painted his series of Charing Cross Bridge; part of the bridge is seen on the right. The young plane trees on the recently completed Embankment had not yet obscured the view.

Monet's painting trips to London over the next two years were all carefully geared to this understanding of the process involved. The first time he went *en famille*, with Alice and Germaine; from then on he always went alone, staying at the Savoy and relying on the rather erratic Michel as interpreter. He saw quite a number of his friends in London, including cosmopolitan Americans such as Whistler, Sargent and Henry James, with whom he watched Queen Victoria's funeral in 1901. One great advantage of the Savoy was that its river frontage featured glassed-in sun balconies, so that Monet was able when painting to combine the visual advantages of *plein-air* painting with indoor comfort.

From the Savoy he continued to paint variations on the two views from his windows down-river towards Waterloo Bridge and up-river towards the Charing Cross railway bridge. The Houses of Parliament, which he had painted from ground level on his first trip to London in 1871, were distantly present in the up-river views. However, Monet rapidly decided that he wanted to paint them in more detail, or rather so that they featured much larger in the composition. With this in mind, he negotiated for permission to paint in St Thomas's Hospital. He soon fell into the routine of painting from the Savoy in the morning and early afternoon, then transferring to St

Thomas's as sunset approached. Despite social distractions he was working well. By 1 March he had started 44 paintings, three days later it was 50 and by 18 March about 65. When he returned to Giverny on 7 April, he brought back some 80 paintings in various stages of completion.

The following year Monet was back at the Savoy in January, but he was forced to begin with pastel sketches while he waited for his crates of canvases to be released by Customs. He began with the Waterloo Bridge paintings (about 10 of them), but he found he was working very slowly, and the weather was capricious (though its fluctuations seem to have been largely in his own over-sensitive imagination), so that soon he had taken up the Charing Cross paintings again. By March he complained that he could not contrive to work on the same motif for even two days in a row, so he resigned himself to the necessity of working in his studio with the merest notations made on the spot.

Monet had to cut short his working time in London during 1901 because of illness and returned to Giverny very depressed. In 1903 he wrote to Durand-Ruel:

> No, I'm not in London except in thought; I'm working steadily on the paintings, which are giving me a lot of trouble. I cannot send you even one London painting because, for the kind of work I am doing, it is vital to have them all before me at once, and in truth not one of them is definitively finished. I work on them all together, or at least a sizeable group of them, and I have no idea yet how many I shall be able to show, as what I am doing to them at the moment is very delicate. One day I feel satisfied, and the next day everything looks bad again. But at least there have to be several that are good.

He was not ready for the London paintings to be shown until May 1904, three years after he had returned from London for the last time. Then a show of 37 of them opened at Durand-Ruel's, and the response was almost universally ecstatic. But by that time Monet himself had moved on. A great deal more had been happening in Giverny than the slow bringing to completion of his pictures from London.

GIVERNY: THE GARDEN

LEFT: **The Artist's Garden at Giverny, 1900.** *Until 1892 Monet and the sons of the family constructed and tended the garden themselves, aided only by occasional hired labour. The area in front of the house was densely planted in blocks and banks of strong colour. Later, the mature garden with its lavish plantings and elaborate juxtapositions of colour, shape, and texture required the services of six gardeners.*

MONET LOVED GIVERNY FROM the start. In October 1890, when it came up for sale, he had confided to Durand-Ruel that 'leaving Giverny would upset me greatly'. So he had decided to take the plunge: the asking price of 22,000 francs was not beyond his resources; he therefore paid it and signed the purchase contract on 17 November. 'I would never find a similarly advantageous situation, or such a beautiful place.'

Once he felt permanently settled, he could think about devoting time and money to the development of the property. It was clearly necessary to enlarge and improve the house as the children were older and required more space and privacy: in 1890 Jean Monet was 23 and Michel 12, while Marthe Hoschedé was 26, Blanche 25, Suzanne 22, Jacques 21, Germaine 17 and Jean-Pierre 13, all of them unmarried and at home, save for Jean, who was doing his military service. But also the grounds had possibilities. During the 1880s a beginning had been made with making the section nearest the house into a flower garden, but much of the land was still put to practical use, to grow vegetables, or allowed to run wild, as a meadow-cum-paddock.

When Monet first moved into the house, the flower garden was already laid out, as a traditional *clos normand* – a formal arrangement with a central path running up from the gate on to the lower road to the main entrance of the house, and symmetrical

BELOW: *Monet in his Giverny garden, 1923–24. The rose arch on the left was the subject of many of his paintings.*

borders on either side with pine trees beyond. Monet clearly did not object to the geometrical layout of the garden as he found it: indeed he painted several pictures of it, almost as though to indicate that he was a master of formal perspective if he wanted to be. After some argument with Alice, he decided to clear most of the shrubs, leaving only the pair of pines flanking the entrance to the house, and put up flimsy metal arches over the central walk on which rambling roses could climb.

Work on the garden at Giverny picked up considerable once Monet owned the property. Spending more time at home, he took much more interest in the scene outside his windows. As social life in Giverny developed, notably with the arrival of the American art colony around 1889–90, there was more and more entertaining, and in the summer months more use of the garden. Monet acquired the services of a gardener, and he began to think more ambitiously. A crucial moment came in February 1893 (at the start of his second period of painting in Rouen), when he bought an irregular plot of land on the other side of the lower road, the Route des Rois, outside his front gate. This section was separated from the clos normand by the road and the small branch railway; it had a river – hardly more than a rivulet – the Ru, a tributary of the Epte, running through it.

At once Monet set about transforming this extra area of land into a water garden, which he wanted to link to the main body of his property by a narrow passage under the road. The new work that he envisaged included damming the Epte to make a large pool intended for water-lilies, and the building of a small footbridge in the Japanese style at one end. There were protracted difficulties with getting the necessary permits to do the work, for which Monet first applied from Rouen. He had to produce

ABOVE: *Monet with his head gardener Félix Breuil and one of the under-gardeners. Monet still directed every aspect of the design and care of his garden and he and Breuil had an uneasy relationship. Brueil's despair following serious floods, which he thought had destroyed the lily-pond, almost drove Monet to suicide.*

LEFT: *On their arrival at Giverny the impecunious family still owned four boats. These were often set adrift by the hostile locals, and the building of a boathouse was an early priority. Following the construction of the lily-pond one gardener was employed full-time in its care. For much of the time he worked from a skiff as shown in the photograph.*

justification for his intentions, and assurances to the locals that growing such purely decorative plants as lilies in the basin would not poison the water supply, before he finally obtained consent in July.

The work was mainly done in the latter half of 1893 – punctuated by frequent cries to Durand-Ruel for advances to pay for it. By January the excavation was complete and the Japanese bridge in place, as can be seen from Monet's first painting of it, done apparently immediately before he set out on his trip to Norway. It was a bitterly cold winter in France, and Monet fussed from Norway about the possible effects of the pond freezing over. As soon as he got back he painted the Japanese bridge again and, now that the waterworks were finished for the moment and the major planting done, he left the new garden to mature. He was, in any case, sufficiently occupied with his series of *Mornings on the Seine*, his excursion to the

LEFT: **The Water-lily Pond and the Bridge: Harmony in Green, 1899.** *The bridge is seen here soon after it was built, before it became covered with wisteria.*

LEFT: **The Rose Arches, Giverny, 1913.** *Some idea of the size and scale of Monet's plantings can be imagined from this spectacular view of the series of rose arches reflected in the water.*

Channel coast and, possibly, his plans for London. Certainly he did not turn seriously to the water garden as a subject until 1898, when he started a group of pictures of the pond, finished and dated the next year.

Compared with his later works on the same theme, these paintings are reasonably explicit, but already he seems in some subtle way to have been reaching towards abstraction. Like the contemporary canvases he painted at the time of a short return visit to Vétheuil (he had a hazy scheme of returning to the major painting locations of his younger days to see what he made of them in his late fifties), most of the water-lily paintings in this batch are nearly square. None of them has a skyline and the sky is present, if at all, only as reflection in the pond. Although the paintings undoubtedly evoke the open air, their effect is curiously enclosed, and with their heavy, overall application of pigment it is not surprising that they have been likened in their effect to tapestries.

With the *Nymphéas* (the botanical name for the kind of water-lily Monet was depicting), he was working from an external reality created by him and carefully set up – this was part of his originality as a gardener – to look like a picture. Likewise, the whole relationship of the Japanese bridge (so-called because of Monet's passion for Japanese prints) to the water-lily pool was calculated in terms of pictorial composition, which fell into position from certain pre-determined viewpoints. It was in a way a method of reducing or eliminating the element of chance from his pictures, if not by confining it to his imagination, then the next best thing: constructing his imaginative landscape on his own doorstep, so that he could have it to hand whenever he wanted it.

RIGHT: *The Japanese collector Madame Kuroki with Monet, Blanche and Lily Butler on the Japanese bridge. The new superstructure was added to support the creeping wisteria.*

Whether in the more formal upper garden or the lower landscape garden, his colour effects were graded with as much care as though he were mixing pigments on his own palette. Moreover, the choice of plants, particularly the water plants, was tied in with the paintings in his head, the shapes and shades he already knew would make satisfactory pictures. When the dealer René Gimpel saw Giverny for the first time in 1918, he was bowled over just by the more formal upper garden:

> I regret my complete ignorance of the names of flowers, as I should like here to name the varieties I saw. A Maeterlinck would be needed for a garden like this. It resembles no other, first because it consists only of the simplest flowers and then because they grow to unheard-of heights. I believe that none is under three feet high. Certain flowers, some of which are white and others yellow, resembling large daisies, shoot up to six feet. It's not a meadow, but a virgin forest of flowers whose colours are very pure, neither pink nor bluish, but red or blue.

In 1901 Monet acquired some more land on the other side of the road. He tripled the length of the lily-pond and then added various details that were to be significant in his paintings, notably the wisteria trellis over the bridge and the thickets of bamboo on the river bank. Having by this time re-formed nature according to the dictates he followed in his art, he settled to painting what he had made. The amount of work he did at this time was prodigious, even for him. He began, according to his own estimate, some 150 pictures of the water garden between 1903 and 1907. He finished 80 of them and showed 48 with Durand-Ruel in 1907.

The effect of the garden on Monet was liberating, but it was also constraining. Possibly this was one of the reasons why Monet felt the need for a change and for this he had gone to London. He may also have felt that, as he entered his sixties, he should get about and partake of experiences while he could still easily do so. Time enough to concentrate on his own garden

ABOVE: **Wisteria**. *A woodblock print by Hiroshige from the series* One Hundred Famous Views in Edo, c.1857. *This and similar prints were a clear source of inspiration for Monet and for his friend Whistler, also a keen connoisseur of Japanese art.*

when it was all he could really manage. Some of his later travelling was purely as a tourist: he went to Spain in 1904, for instance, specifically to see the Prado and the works of Velázquez, which were at that time very popular and much discussed. His visit to Venice with Alice late in 1908, however, was undoubtedly designed as a painting trip to introduce a welcome variety into his work. There is something slightly dutiful, however, about his pictures from the Venice trip. They are, of course, conventionally ravishing in colour, but depict only the most obvious tourist attractions, such as San Marco, San Giorgio and so on. Monet was producing, in a way he never had before, what was expected rather than what he personally was driven to do.

By 1908 Monet was nearing 70. He had begun to have trouble with his eyesight, a premonition of the cataracts that were later to become acute. Alice was only four years younger, and the photographs of them together in Venice show them as old, overweight and clearly not in the best of health. Immediately on their return Alice was taken ill and had to spend long periods in bed before she was sufficiently recovered for the household to return to normal. Venice was Monet's last significant excursion as a painter outside his own close circle of Giverny.

In 1910 it became evident that, after a period of remission, Alice's condition – a type of leukaemia – was terminal. That winter she took to her bed again and never left it until her death on 19 May 1911. After Alice's death, and her funeral, at which there was a large last gathering of old friends, including Degas, now almost blind and able to get about only with a stick, Monet was in every sense desolated. He was moody and depressed, and for some months he was unable to work at all. Finally, by the end of the year, he decided he had to work again and took up the long-neglected products of his time in Venice. These of course brought back

ABOVE: *Monet and Alice feeding the pigeons in St Mark's Square, Venice, 1908. This was the last foreign visit either was to make.*

RIGHT: **Palazzo da Mula, Venice, 1908**. *Perhaps lacking the stimulus of his beloved and intimately understood garden, Monet's views of Venice reveal a detachment that never quite allows them to rise above the touristic.*

painful memories of Alice. As he wrote to his stepdaughter Germaine, 'We were so happy together during our stay there; she was so proud of my burning energy.' In the new year he confided to Durand-Ruel:

> As for me, I am still dragging myself sadly along. These festive days have been really painful for me to get through, and as a result I feel doubly sad, battered and completely discouraged. Still, I have just taken a grip on myself and again taken up my neglected brushes: I hope I shall soon have finished the Venice canvases.

Although Monet had brought back from Venice 37 canvases, and had arranged for their exclusive exhibition with the dealer Bernheim-Jeune, he had not initially hurried to unpack them and get on with their completion. After Alice died, he was too upset, and in any case he had too much else to look after to take up work on them again. Consequently the long-promised showing did not take place until May 1912, when 29 of the 37 were shown, to universal acclaim.

A few days before the show opened Monet wrote, with unusual frankness even for him, to Durand-Ruel:

> If for so long you have found me profoundly discontented with what I have been doing, that's because that has been how I really think. More than ever, I realize how little all the undeserved success I have had really counts. I always hope to do better, but age and pain have drained my strength. I know perfectly well in advance that you will judge my paintings perfect. I know that, if they are shown, they will have a great success, but I couldn't care less, since I know they are bad; I'm sure of it.

Another personal tragedy now arose. His son Jean, after his marriage to Blanche Hoschedé in 1897 (already disquieting to his father, who worried about whether he really loved the girl or was just acquiescing to her wishes), had gone to work in Rouen. Now ill with a brain tumour, Jean died

ABOVE: *A photograph of Monet at work in July 1915, shaded by an umbrella from the sun. He is attended by the faithful Blanche and his step-grand-daughter Nitia Salerou. Blanche, having been a painter herself, was well able to help with the changing of canvases and provision of paints.*

in his father's house in February 1914. Blanche decided to give up all her own artistic ambitions to move in and keep house for Monet. As he himself recognized, he was very difficult, and he found Blanche's care and attention for him as touching as it was inexplicable.

The death of Jean was not the end of his woes. The trouble with his eyesight, which had begun to manifest itself at around the time of the Venice trip, was becoming acute. Distrusting any ideas of surgery for the moment, he found his own way of dealing with the problem: he began to paint much bigger. Up to 1908 the very largest of the *Nymphéas* canvases reached 100 x 100 centimetres and that was exceptional. The first of the *Nymphéas* he began to work on in 1914, immediately after Jean's death, were significantly larger, and from then on most of the major *Nymphéas* series were very large indeed, whether they were individual canvases or conceived as diptychs or triptychs. He himself observed that if he could still work with his own eyes, it was only because of the size he was now

LEFT: *Monet working by the lily-pond on the* Nymphéas *series in about 1920. The entire household revolved around Monet and his dedication to his work – woe betide the staff or family if meals were not punctual.*

Monet's Eyesight

A REMARKABLE NUMBER of artists in the nineteenth century seem to have suffered from disorders of the eye – or maybe it was just that advances in medicine made doctors and sufferers more aware of such things and eager to find a solution. Some painters appear not to have necessarily conceived them as disadvantages: when Cézanne was offered spectacles for his myopia, he replied, 'Take these vulgar things away', while Monet in a similar situation tried the spectacles on, then handed them back with, 'My God, I'm seeing just like Bouguereau'. (Bouguereau was a successful academic painter of the period whose immaculately smooth, detailed nudes were particularly detested and derided by the Impressionists.)

Sometimes these sight difficulties and their supposed effects in shaping Impressionist style backfired on painters who did not recognize the problem. Huysmans, in general a fairly sympathetic critic, did not much approve of Cézanne and once described him as 'an artist with a diseased retina, who, exasperated by a defective vision, discovered the basis of a new art.' Jules Ferry said in 1906 that Cézanne was 'an incomplete talent, in which imperfect vision resulted in work that was always incomplete and sketchy.' Also, the eye conditions tended to get worse: the myopia of Renoir and Degas (along with corneal ulcers) led eventually to blindness in both cases, and a concentration instead on sculpture. Pissarro, also myopic, was in his last years too morbidly sensitive to light to work outdoors.

LEFT: *Monet in 1923 recovering from his first, unsuccessful, operation to remove cataracts.*

Monet's problems with his eyes are more famous than those of the other Impressionists, principally because he was successfully treated for them and left detailed accounts of their effect before and after. Although he seems to have long suffered from a degree of myopia, the serious problems with cataracts did not manifest themselves until his trip to Venice in 1908, when he was nearly 70. Almost as soon as cataracts were diagnosed, an operation was suggested, but he was wary. Half a century earlier Daumier had been operated on unsuccessfully, and Monet certainly knew of the inconclusive results in the case of his fellow Impressionist Mary Cassatt. Also, owing to the limitations of anaesthetics currently available, the operation was difficult and painful.

In 1918 Monet told the critic Thibault-Sisson of his sufferings in the previous few years:

I no longer saw colours so intensely, I no longer painted light so accurately. Reds looked muddy to me, pinks insipid, and the intermediate or lower tones escaped me altogether. On the other hand, forms always came across quite clearly and I rendered them as decisively as ever. At first I tried to hold out. How often I have stayed for hours by this little bridge here, under the harshest sun, sitting on my camp stool, under my parasol, and forced myself to take up again my interrupted work and try to recapture the freshness that had vanished from my palette. Wasted efforts. My painting got darker and darker, more and more like an Old Master, and, when I was done and compared the results to earlier work, I was thrown into such a rage of frustration that I would slash all my canvases to shreds with my penknife.

In consequence, Monet decided to have the operation in 1922. The first operation in the following year was quite successful but, as Monet's surgeon predicted, a second was soon required. Monet was bitterly disappointed, believing that he had been misled and would never again regain his sight. However, the second operation was carried out successfully, improving his sight enormously, even though he now saw everything too yellow, and the disparity between his eyes made it impossible for him to work with both eyes open together. But in 1924 he was put in contact with Professor Jacques Mawas, who seems to have been something of a virtuoso in the prescription of spectacles. When Monet first met the Professor, who came down to Giverny with Clemenceau, he told him:

> I see blue. I no longer see red or yellow. This irritates me terribly because I know the colours exist. I know that on my palette there is some red, some yellow, a special green and a certain violet. I can no longer see them as I used to, but I recall very well the colours they gave me.

Mawas made for Monet a variety of different lenses, tinted and untinted. As a result of the new lenses Monet soon overcame this dominance of blue, and by July 1925 he was writing to his friend André Barbier:

> Since your last visit my sight is unthinkably improved. I am working harder than ever, am pleased with what I am doing, and if the new glasses are even better I would like to live to be a hundred.

In fact he had another two years of continuous and often impassioned activity, after a peiod during which he could work only on a large scale. He also had experienced severe problems in seeing blue, which the operation finally resolved. Had it not been for the advances in contemporary medicine he might by then have been blind, and those amazing last works would never have come into existence.

BELOW: **The House, Giverny, c.1922.** *Monet's inability to distinguish colours has left us a number of oils with startling bold forms and dramatically narrow colour range.*

painting. In 1914 Clemenceau managed to encourage him to develop an idea that had been at the back of his mind for some time: a scheme of decoration based on the *Nymphéas*, conceived on an heroic scale and destined for some grand public purpose. Monet was so excited by the idea that he at once started building a large studio block to the east of the house, further extended and completed in 1916, despite the difficult wartime conditions. It was designed so that he could work on the large canvases of the garden and, especially, as the scheme formed in his mind, on the *Grandes Décorations*.

Throughout the First World War, Monet struggled on with the decorations and other water-lily paintings. His eyesight was still deteriorating, but he was unusually economical with complaints, perhaps realizing that the troubles of the world at large placed such matters in perspective. Military call-up had reduced the number of gardeners (which had previously reached five in addition to the head gardener, Félix Breuil), and the produce of the vegetable garden was mainly set aside for a military hospital that had been set up on a neighbouring property. Clemenceau was as attentive and supportive as ever of his old friend, surprisingly so since as a statesman he was busier than ever during the war, and was even Prime Minister for a period. In 1916 Monet was intensely worried by the knowledge that his son Michel was at Verdun through the worst of the fighting, though fortunately he escaped without injury. Jean-Pierre Hoschedé also came through the war unscathed.

As things became a little less problematic at home, Monet started to move around a little more. In October 1917 Degas's death moved Monet to make one of his rare visits to Paris for the funeral. Immediately afterwards Monet and Blanche left on a trip lasting a couple of weeks to the Normandy coast of his childhood, a visit to Honfleur, Le Havre and Dieppe. Monet realized that he needed the break and in any case longed to see the sea again, as he had

BELOW: *A photograph of Monet during the first World War, when his younger son and step-sons were at the front, his old friends dying and his eyesight steadily failing.*

not set eyes on it for a long time. In August 1918 he refused an invitation to stay from the dealer Gustave Bernheim-Jeune, noting:

> It's very kind of you to ask us, and it would give Blanche and me a great deal of pleasure. But I have never been less inclined to take any time off from my painting. I don't have many years left to me, and I have to devote all my time to painting, in the hope of achieving something worthwhile in the end, something that might possibly satisfy even me.

On the eve of the Armistice in 1918 he wrote about the *Grandes Décorations* to Clemenceau, who had been closely involved with the scheme for some time:

BELOW: *Monet in his new studio at Giverny. This was built, despite the privations of the war, to house the* Grandes Décorations.

ABOVE: **Water Lilies: Study of Water – The Clouds, 1922-26.** *A triptych of the Nymphéas series. These huge canvases were installed in the Musée de l'Orangerie in 1927, after Monet's death.*

I am just about to put the finishing touches to two decorative panels, which I want to sign on Victory day itself. I am writing to ask you if they might be given to the state, through your mediation. It's not very much but it is the only way I have of participating in the victory. I'd like the panels to be in the Musée des Arts Décoratifs and would be very happy if you could make the selection.

Although the offer was accepted in principle, this was not the end of the story. Monet was to go on and on working at the series.

As well as the *Nymphéas* in various formats and sizes, Monet painted aspects of the garden nearer to the house, and there are smaller series of irises, wisteria, rose thickets and a variety of water plants. He still painted out of doors in good weather, though he regretted to Bernheim-Jeune during the war that, beautiful though the snow was, he was too old to go out in such cold weather to paint it. In 1919, much to his distress, the last of his old Impressionist friends, Renoir, died. This felt to Monet like the end of an era, and he sensed he had outlived his time. He wrote touchingly to Félix Fénéon:

With him goes a part of my own life ... It's hard to be alone, though no doubt it's not for long, as I'm feeling my age more and more with each day that passes ...

In 1922 he signed the deed of gift presenting the water-lily panels to the nation. (They were finally installed in two galleries of the Orangerie in the Tuileries on 17 May 1927, after Monet's death.) However, his failing eyesight was becoming an acute concern. In 1923, after frequent and anguished consultation with the eye-doctor Charles Coutela, he consented to have a series of operations on his cataracts, at the age of 82.

At first he thought the operation was a disaster, but after two more he realized that, having suffered a great deal of pain, he really could see clearly again. Alarmingly, it was if anything too clearly. He wrote to Clemenceau at the end of August:

The distortion and exaggeration of colours I see is quite terrifying ... If I were condemned to seeing nature always as I see it now, I'd prefer to stay blind and just remember the beauties I have always seen. Still, this will certainly not prove to be the case.

Clemenceau: The 'Tiger' of France

'AS MUCH AS ANY single human being, miraculously magnified, can ever be a nation, Clemenceau was France.' So wrote Winston Churchill in 1930 of Georges Clemenceau, the man who, more than anyone else, emerged in the eyes of the world as the victor of the First World War.

Born in the Vendée, Clemenceau trained as a doctor and was initiated into the intricacies of practical politics as a journalist in New York. He was back in Paris in time for the end of the Second Empire and was then to achieve his first position of consequence on 5 September 1870, the day after the proclamation of the Third Republic, as Mayor of Montmartre. This meant that he held the post during the most bloody days of the Paris Commune. There were few big issues in the Third Republic, from reform of the army to the building of the Panama Canal, in which he did not have a hand, frequently a more important one than might appear from his official position as a member of the Chambre des Deputés. By 1906 he had become leader of the majority party in the Chamber. When the stalemate in the First World War was presented to him in 1917, he revivified the French fighting spirit, turned the home problems of the Germans to the advantage of the Allies and dominated the Versailles Peace Conference. Voted out of office in 1920, in his 80th year, he lived until 1929, remaining a force to reckon with.

He became acquainted with Monet some time in the 1890s and proved himself in 1895 (out of office and returned to journalism) one of the most perceptive critics of Monet's *Cathedrals* show. Both men were both enthusiastic supporters of Alfred Dreyfus, whose conviction for treason and imprisonment caused a scandal in France.

LEFT: *Young Clemenceau in about 1870, when he was Mayor of Montmartre during the Commune.*

RIGHT: *The aged ex-President presides at Monet's funeral, flanked by Blanche, Germaine and Michael.*

In 1899 Monet conferred a rare favour on his friend. Unusually, he presented one of his paintings, The Rock to the famous statesman.

After 1900 Clemenceau was probably Monet's closest friend. He was an enthusiastic proponent of Monet's work, and it was largely through his good offices that the plans for a major public work, the *Nymphéas* rooms in the Orangerie, finally came to fruition. He was also the only person of sufficient stature, and proved affection, to be firm with Monet about the need for an operation for his cataracts. He even wrote a little moral tale for Monet, the title of which translates as *Philosophical Reflections from the Very Lofty on the Very Lowly, or the Marvellous History of a Blind Man who Refused to Open his Eyes*, to reinforce the point.

Clemenceau was at Monet's side when the painter died at Giverny. A year later, in 1928, he published *Claude Monet: Les Nymphéas.*

However, equipped with some new glasses from Germany, he discovered that he could after all see again green, red and even, at last, a faint blue – the colour above all others that cataracts tend to eliminate from the spectrum. He began busily retouching, or sometimes repainting, pictures that had tended excessively towards the hot colours that he had worked on during his days of blunted sight. He painted on to the last, finishing with a group of paintings composed of tumultuous, almost indecipherable, patterns of colour, in which the outline of the house seen from a thicket of roses is just distinguishable.

During these last years Monet became the object of veneration. As his garden recovered from the effects of war and continued to mature, an increasing number of people wanted to pay a visit to the garden and to him. The faithful Blanche helped to guard his privacy against all but the most favoured, and usually oldest, friends. His paintings during this time indicate a unique concentration: with virtually no other subject matter to distract him and dissipate his artistic energies, Monet painted himself deeper and deeper into his one obsessive subject: the garden, with its waters and its plants. The water-lilies were not individual plants in a particular garden: he reduced them to the essential idea of a water-lily and, beyond that, to a series of abstract shapes that can hardly be recognized. The paint was applied ever more thinly, until the pictures seem almost as though painted on silk, and it is only at the end that something of the fury and the heavy impasto of the last Argenteuil pictures returns. And there, if it really is fury, is the titanic anger of an old man faced with death and battling with the failure of those very senses he has always trusted and lived by. The very last of his pictures are profound and uncomfortable.

At the end of his life Monet was a curiously isolated figure. Although he had outlived all the other Impressionists, and every other leading painter in his generation, he had, unlike any of them, gone on developing,

ABOVE: *Monet in the doorway of the second studio at Giverny, photographed by Baron Mayer in October 1905.*

RIGHT: **Self-Portrait,
c.1917.** *Rescued by
Clemenceau, this was one of
four self-portraits that Monet
was encouraged by Blanche to
paint during the harsh winter
of 1917. A perfectionist to
the last, Monet destroyed
the remainder.*

experimenting and questing right to the last. The main difference was that
finally he was accepted as a modern classic and able to command high prices
for his work. The most exacting standard of judgement he had to meet was
his own, and if he did not consistently satisfy that, it was of concern only to
himself; he was universally respected and admired.

On the other hand, he did seem to be in something of a backwater. His
later explorations had taken him in one direction, even as the main stream
of modern art headed in another. While he was increasingly dissolving

form in light, the Post-Impressionists, such as Paul Gauguin, had begun to border it again with hard lines. They filled the areas thus defined with flat, evenly applied colour, so moving totally awy from the *plein-air* effect. The next generation, that of Henri Matisse and the Fauves, developed the Post-Impressionist idea, using ever-more brilliant and non-realistic colours. If any of the Impressionists was exerting a direct influence on the young painters of the 1900s, it was surprisingly not Monet at all, but rather his old friend Cézanne. In his later days Cézanne had become more and more concerned with representing volume – a matter that was of little interest to Monet – and it was this that excited Picasso and Georges Braque. They in turn were to elaborate Analytical Cubism, which employed Cézanne's limited range of brownish Provençal colours and segmented form, to bring the finished painting ever nearer to Abstraction.

Monet's late paintings were to exert their influence, but not until some 20 years after his death. By then it was Cubism that looked like a spent force. Painters were more interested in instinctive, unconcious responses than in analyzing what they saw before them. In New York and Paris they began painting in an abstract style so emotional and informal in its splashing and swirling of colour across the canvas that it was soon termed Abstract Expressionism. The colours themselves might have more to do with the brilliant Fauve palette, but the formal sense and construction of the paintings took up exactly where Monet's latest and most profoundly abstracted evocations of water lilies had left off.

Loaded with honours, revered at last by all, Monet died on 6 December 1926, three weeks after his 86th birthday. He was the last Impressionist, the last of an heroic generation, who followed his own way and, despite financial and critical success, was never completely confident or satisfied. He was, finally, always alone in his private world. He thought that he was recording nature, but in the end he tore nature apart and remoulded it in the privacy of his own imagination, as art.

IN THE FOOTSTEPS OF MONET

EVEN TODAY, FRANCE SEEMS an expansive country. Less populated in Monet's day and relatively late to feel the pressures of industrialization, its varied climate and dramatic changes of terrain provided a rich source of motifs to which Monet could respond. However, the regions he most frequently chose to paint (as shown on the map opposite) were the landscapes of the Seine valley between Paris and his Normandy childhood home, and the Channel coasts on either side of the Seine estuary. The map also reveals what a study of his *oeuvre* confirms: that he preferred to find a place and a motif to examine over time and capture in paint, so that the eventual canvases become the distilled visual experience of that place.

In spite of this deliberately restricted choice of locality, the body of Monet's work makes us feel a sense of recognition, of having ourselves visited the familiar scenes of Monet's France. The passionate attention with which he viewed and recorded his surroundings vividly evokes that now almost vanished world of peasant agriculture, even then under threat by processes of historical change. The sensation of presence is powerful, whether the landscape recorded is the spectacle of Paris during its years of most violent and creative upheaval and transformation; or the Normandy coast, with its moods of sunshine and sudden storm; the craggy and wild terrain of remote central France, for which the valley of the Creuse is a key symbol; or the sun-drenched Riviera with its flat-roofed houses and African vegetation, coloured earth and brilliant light; or the moods of his beloved River Seine – sunlit, misty, autumnal, frozen – and its string of changing towns and villages. Most important of all these sites is Monet's own place, the garden he created at Giverny, of which such an intimate visual record was left that it has been possible to restore it after forty years' neglect.

Although Paris has changed almost beyond recognition, many of the places associated with Monet remain to be visited. First among these is the Maison du Pressoir at Giverny. This is now administered by the Fondation Claude Monet, in association with the Académie des Beaux-Arts who have supervised the renovation of the house and gardens. Monet's collection of Japanese art is still in place, and some of his paintings are on loan from private collections (others can be seen in the nearby Musée Alphonse Poulain at Vernon). For further information contact the Fondation Claude Monet, Giverny, Eure (tel: 32 51 28 21). The house and its collection of Monet's paintings (his own and those of his friends) was bequeathed to the Académie by Michel Monet in 1966; he did not want them left to the State which had treated his father with such little respect before the years of his great fame. The house was in too poor a state to leave the paintings *in situ*; they were therefore removed to the Musée du Marmottan in Paris, which is administered by the Académie (Musée du Marmottan, 2 rue de Louis Boilly, 75016 Paris. Tel: (1) 42 24 07 02). Separate from its general collections, the museum houses a permanent exhibition entitled 'Monet and his Friends'.

However, the State does hold the major collection of Monet's work and that of his contemporaries, now housed in the Musée d'Orsay (1 rue de Bellechasse, Quai d'Orsay, 75007 Paris. Tel: (1) 40 49 48 14). The core of this, the richest collection of Impressionist work in France, is Caillebotte's bequest, accepted so reluctantly by the State authorities. Also in Paris is the permanent display of the *Grandes Décorations*, the *Nymphéas*, in the pavilions of the Musée de l'Orangerie close to the Louvre (Jardin des Tuileries, 75001 Paris. Tel: (1) 42 97 48 16). This museum also houses Impressionist works collected by Walter Guillaume, principally by Renoir.

Other places of interest include the Musée de l'Ile de France at Sceaux, , the Musée Fabre in Montpellier and the Musée des Beaux-Arts in Rouen. The Musée Eugène Boudin at Honfleur contains works with an interesting early influence on Monet.

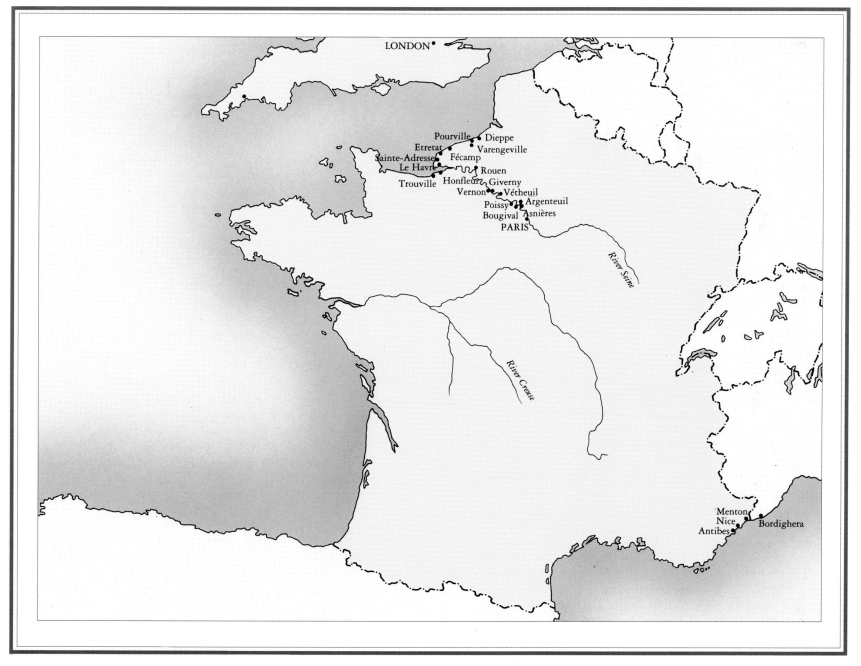

LONDON

Pourville Dieppe
Etretat Varengeville
Sainte-Adresse Fécamp
Le Havre Rouen
Trouville Honfleur Giverny
Vernon Vétheuil
Poissy Argenteuil
Bougival Asnières
PARIS

River Seine

River Creuse

Menton
Nice Bordighera
Antibes

$\mathcal{F}$RIENDS AND ACQUAINTANCES

BAZILLE, Jean-Frédéric *(1841–1870)* The friendship of Bazille, combined with his help in providing financial support and studio-space, were the essential props of Monet's early career. Bazille's work and Monet's shared many characteristics during the 1860s; both were painters of figures in the open air, and of still-lifes. However, Bazille's career was cut short by his early death in the Franco-Prussian War.

BOUDIN, Eugène *(1824–1898)* Boudin painted the Normandy coast around his native Honfleur almost exclusively. He first met Monet in 1856 and they frequently worked together during the 1860s. Boudin's freely styled studies of bourgeois summer visitors to the coast were innovative and influenced Monet's treatment of similar motifs. Late in life Monet claimed he owed everything to the older painter's advice to paint from nature in the open air.

CAILLEBOTTE, Gustave *(1848–1894)* A wealthy painter introduced to the Impressionist circle by Degas, Caillebotte collected many of their early works, including several by Monet. His patronage was instrumental in enabling several of the group to develop and succeed, and his tireless energy was the driving force of the early Impressionist exhibitions. A talented painter himself, he combined many of Monet's motifs, including gardens and boating, with Degas' innovative use of perspective in portraying bourgeois city life. He bequeathed his matchless collection to the State, which was reluctant to accept it, partly as a result of the anarchist outrages of previous years which several *avant-garde* artists had supported. Monet joined Pissarro and others in the three-year campaign that led to the paintings' eventual acceptance.

CEZANNE, Paul *(1839–1906)* Monet and Cézanne met in 1860 and became close friends. The latter worked with Pissarro and showed with the Impressionists in the early years, but his interests later moved beyond Impressionism towards an exploration of pictorial structure. After moving to his native Provence he continued to maintain links with Monet; they held one another in high regard and each owned several of the other's paintings. Like Monet with his garden, Cézanne endlessly re-worked one motif in his art: that of the Mont St Victoire.

CLEMENCEAU, Georges *(1841–1929)* The major political figure in the France of Monet's lifetime, he forged a remarkable friendship with the painter and was active in many campaigns in the Arts and in support of artists. He would seem to have inspired Monet to paint the great series of Nymphéas for the Musée de l'Orangerie, and his efforts to ensure they were completed threatened a break in their relations. However, it was largely due to his encouragement that Monet's eyesight was saved. Clemenceau travelled to Giverny to be at Monet's deathbed in 1926.

DEGAS, Edgar *(1834–1917)* A leading Impressionist whose work was closer to that of Manet than Monet, both in style and in the predominance of urban and social themes in his subject matter. The two men greatly admired one another in spite of sometimes vociferous differences of opinion; Degas' late pastels of landscape, executed when his eyesight was failing, show Monet's influence.

DELACROIX, Eugène *(1798–1863)* The leading exponent of the Romantic tradition in France, his work was noted for its brilliant colour and rejection of academic and classical tradition. The young Impressionists championed his reputation in opposition to his contemporary and rival Jacques-Louis David, the leading Neo-classicist of the nineteenth century. Delacroix's long struggle with the art establishment for official recognition and acceptance by the Salon was echoed in the Impressionists' own.

DURAND-RUEL, Paul *(1831–1922)* A dealer whose early admiration for Impressionism at times threatened to bankrupt him, he was Monet's principal agent and collector. He also acted as his banker in the early years of desperate poverty. However, their relationship was often tortured; Monet could be disloyal, and in the 1890s the two men had a major disagreement about the sale of Monet's works to American collectors, which ironically became the main source of Monet's subsequent wealth. Nevertheless a *rapprochement* followed, ensuring that Monet's old patron was the first to show the series paintings as a group.

GOGH, Theodore van *(1857–1891)* A keen supporter of *avant-garde* painters, Vincent's brother Theo was agent for the fashionable gallery Boussod and Valadon. In this capacity he helped Monet to survive the rift with Durand-Ruel whilst also raising the price of his paintings; uniquely, Monet had a contract with them for 1888–89, when Theo took ten of Monet's *Antibes* canvases for exhibition.

HOSCHEDE-MONET, Alice *(1844–1911)* Born Alice Raingo, a considerable heiress, she married Ernest Hoschedé. Alice brought up Monet's two sons with her own six children at Vétheuil and Poissy, then at Giverny, showing considerable fortitude during the early years of privation, debt, and enforced moves and separations. She and Monet were finally married quietly in 1892.

JONGKIND, Johan Barthold *(1819–1891)* A Dutch artist, primarily of landscapes, who was active around le Havre and much admired by the young Monet. Although Jongkind was not truly a *plein-air* painter, he worked with Monet and Boudin from the Ferme St Siméon at Honfleur and showed with them at the Salon des Refusés in 1863.

MANET, Edouard *(1832–1883)* Already a controversial artist whilst Monet was still a student, Manet's bold technical and stylist experiments and unconventional subject matter strongly influenced the emerging school. However, Manet never exhibited with the Impressionists. Following Manet's death, Monet organized the purchase of his *Olympia* for the State and led the campaign for its acceptance by the Louvre.

MONET, Camille *(1847-1879)* Seventeen-year-old Camille Doncieux modelled for the student Monet in Paris. After several years of often clandestine co-habitation and the birth of their son Jean in 1867, they were married in 1870. Poverty and deprivation ruined her health, and she died in 1879 soon after the birth of Michel. She appears in many of Monet's early figure paintings.

MORISOT, Berthe *(1841–1895)* An early *protegée* of Manet, she later married his brother Eugène, partly to ensure a professional and social freedom denied to single women of her class. Morisot studied with Corot and was a fully accepted member of the Impressionist group, exhibiting in all their collective shows. She maintained close links with Monet and Renoir as well as Manet which can be discerned in the evolution of their respective work. Monet arranged her retrospective show at Durand-Ruel following her untimely death.

PISSARRO, Camille *(1830–1903)* Part Jewish, a passionate political radical and the oldest artist of the Impressionist group, Pissarro was its most dedicated supporter of their collective shows. His relations with Monet soured following disputes in the 1880s over the inclusion of Pissarro's *protegés*. The rift healed following their mutual defence of Dreyfus in 1894. In the early years he joined *plein-air* expeditions with Renoir, Monet, Cézanne and the young Gauguin; Pissarro also introduced Monet to Durand-Ruel in London during their exile in the Franco-Prussian War. From the 1890s he adhered to the new Pointillist technique advocated by Seurat.

RENOIR, Pierre-Auguste *(1841–1919)* Of all the Impressionists, Renoir was closest to Monet and their friendship was enduring. In the early years they worked closely together, both in Paris and on the Seine north of the capital. Monet later avoided joint expeditions, claiming that disputes over technique distracted him from painting. They last met in 1908 at Cagnes, Renoir's Riviera home, as Monet returned from Venice.

RODIN, Auguste *(1840–1917)* France's most important sculptor in the nineteenth century, his work has been described as a three-dimensional equivalent of Impressionist painting. However, Rodin's radical employment of fragmentation techniques and 'unfinished' appearance to express an emotional reality make him more properly the heir to the Romantic tradition. Of the group, he was closest to Monet and shared the triumphal success of their joint show at Georges Petit's gallery in 1889; he too encountered much opposition from the artistic establishment.

MUSEUM AND GALLERY CREDITS

Works are by Claude Monet unless otherwise stated.

FRONT COVER: *The Poppies at Argenteuil*, 1873. Oil, 50 x 65 cm (19.7 x 25.6 in). Musée d'Orsay, Paris. TITLE PAGE: *View of Rouen*, c.1883. Black crayon on scratchboard, 32.6 x 49.5 cm (12.8 x 19.5 in). Sterling and Francine Clark Art Institute, Williamstown. FRONTISPIECE: *The Dock at Argenteuil*, 1872. Oil, 60 x 80.5 cm (23.6 x 31.7 in). Musée de l'Orangerie, Paris.

INTRODUCTION
p6 *Self-Portrait of the Artist Wearing a Beret*, 1886. Oil, 56 x 46 cm (22 x 18 in). At Giverny; Document Galerie Robert Schmit, Paris. p7 *The Petite Creuse*, 1888–89. Oil, 65.9 x 93.1 cm (26 x 36.6 in). Art Institute of Chicago (Mr & Mrs Potter Palmer Collection 1922).

CHAPTER 1
p10 *Farmyard in Normandy*, c.1863. Oil, 65 x 80 cm (25.5 x 31.5 in). Musée d'Orsay, Paris. p12 Left: Sheet of caricatures: *People of the Theatre*, c.1856. Black chalk and gouache, 34 x 48 cm (13.4 x 18.9 in). Musée Marmottan, Paris. Right: *Man with a Large Nose*, 1855–56. Graphite on tan paper, 24.9 x 15.2 cm (9.8 x 6 in). Art Institute of Chicago (Gift of Carter H. Harrison 1933). p13 *Caricature of François-Charles Ochard*, c.1855–56. Graphite on buff paper, 31.8 x 24.6 cm (12.5 x 9.7 in). Art Institute of Chicago (Gift of Mr & Mrs Carter H. Harrison 1933). p15 *The Green Wave*, 1865. Oil, 48.6 x 64.8 cm (19.1 x 25.5 in). Metropolitan Museum of Art, New York (H.O. Havermeyer Collection, gift of Mrs H.O. Havermeyer). p18 *Village Road in Normandy (rue de la Bavolle, Honfleur)*, 1864. Oil, 58 x 63 cm (22.8 x 24.8 in). Stadtische Kunsthalle, Mannheim. p19 The *Pointe de la Hève at Low Tide*, 1865. Oil, 90.2 x 150.5 cm (35.5 x 59.25 in). Kimbell Art Museum, Fort Worth Texas.

CHAPTER 2
p22 *The Beach at Sainte-Adresse*, 1867. Oil, 75.8 x 102.5 cm (29.8 x 40.35 in). Art Institute of Chicago (Mr & Mrs Lewis Larned Coburn Memorial Collection 1933). p23 Left: Xylograph caricature by Grandville, 1844. From *Une Autre Monde* (Bibliothèque Nationale, Paris). p27 *The Mouth of the Seine at Honfleur*, 1865. Oil, 90 x 150 cm (35.4 x 59 in). The Norton Simon Art Foundation, Pasadena. p30 Drawing by Eugène Boudin: *Painters at the Ferme St Siméon*, 1863. Collection Galerie Robert Schmit, Paris. p31 *The Quai du Louvre*, 1867. Oil, 65 x 93 cm (25.6 x 36.6 in). Haags Gemeente-museum, Rotterdam. p35 *The Road from Chailly to Fontainebleau (le Pavé de Chailly)*, 1864. Oil, 98 x 130 cm (38.5 x 51 in). Private Collection, Paris; Document Archives Durand-Ruel. p36 Edouard Manet: *Portrait of Berthe Morisot*, c.1872. Lithograph, 19 x 13.5 cm (7.5 x 5.3 in). p38 *Camille: The Woman in the Green Dress*, 1866. Oil, 231 x 151 cm (90.9 x 59 in). Kunsthalle, Bremen. p39 Study for *Déjeuner sur l'herbe (Luncheon on the Grass)*, 1865–6. Oil, 130 x 181 cm (51 x 71.25 in). Pushkin Museum, Moscow. p43 *Bathers at La Grenouillère*, 1869. Oil, 73 x 92 cm (28.7 x 36.2 in). National Gallery, London. p47 *The Terrace at Sainte-Adresse*, 1867. Oil, 98.1 x 129.9 cm (38.6 x 51 in). Metropolitan Museum of Art, New York (purchased with special contributions given or bequeathed by Friends of the Museum 1967).

CHAPTER 3
p50 *Impression, Sunrise*, 1873. Oil, 48 x 63 cm (18.9 x 24.8 in). Musée Marmottan, Paris. p51 *Portrait of a Woman (Camille?)*, c.1868. Red chalk drawing, 28.6 x 21 cm (11.26 x 8.27 in). Private Collection, USA. p54 Edouard Manet: *The Barricade*, 1871. Lithograph, 46 x 33.3 cm (18 x 13 in). p55 *The Train in the Snow: The Locomotive*, 1875. Oil, 59 x 78 cm (23.2 x 30.7 in). Musée Marmottan, Paris (gift of Mme Donop de Monchy). p58 *The Train in the Country*, c.1870–71. Oil, 50 x 65 cm (19.68 x 25.6 in). Musée d'Orsay, Paris. p59 *The Bridge at Argenteuil*, 1874. Oil, 60.5 x 80 cm (23.8 x 31.5 in). Musée d'Orsay, Paris. p63 *Poppies near Vétheuil*, 1880. Oil, 71.5 x 90.5 cm (28 x 35.6 in). E.G. Buhrle Foundation, Zurich. p66 Left: Hokusai: *The Sazaido of the Gohyaku Rakanji Temple* (coloured woodblock print from *Thirty-six Views of Mount Fuji*, c.1850–52. British Museum, London. p66 Hiroshige: Coloured woodblock print of a stormy sea. Victoria & Albert Museum, London. p67 *Camille in Japanese Costume (La Japonaise)*, 1876. Oil, 231.6 x 142.3 cm (91.18 x 56 in). Museum of Fine Arts, Boston (1951 Purchase Fund). p69 Edouard Manet: *Portrait sketch of Monet*, 1874. Pen & ink, 15.2 x 12.7 cm (5.9 x 5 in). Musée Marmottan, Paris. p70 *The Red Cape*, c.1870. Oil, 99 x 79.3 cm (38.9 x 31.2 in). Cleveland Museum of Art, Ohio (Bequest of Leonard C. Hanna Jr). p71 *Camille at the Window, Argenteuil*, 1873. Oil, 60.3 x 49.8 cm (23.7 x 19.6 in).

MUSEUM AND GALLERY CREDITS

Virginia Museum of Fine Arts, Richmond (Collection of Mr & Mrs Paul Mellon). **p74** *Men Unloading Coal*, 1875. Oil, 55 x 66 cm (21.6 x 26 in). Musée d'Orsay, Paris **p75** *Gare St Lazare: Arrival of a Train*, 1877. Oil, 83.1 x 101.5 cm (32.7 x 40 in). Fogg Art Museum, Harvard University Art Museums (Bequest of Maurice Wertheim Class of 1906). **p76–77.** *Gare St Lazare*: 1877, from Monet's sketchbook MM 5128. Pencil, 26 x 34 cm (10.2 x 13.4 in). Musée Marmottan, Paris.

CHAPTER 4
p78 *Ice Floes*, 1880. Oil, 97 x 150.5 cm (38 x 59.25 in). Shelburne Museum, Vermont (photo by Ken Burns). **p82** *The Artist's Garden at Vétheuil*, 1880. Oil, 151.4 x 121 cm (59.6 x 47.6 in). National Gallery of Art, Washington (Ailsa Mellon Bruce Collection). **p83** *Hoarfrost near Vétheuil (Le Givre)*, 1880. Oil, 61 x 100 cm (24 x 39.4 in). Musée d'Orsay, Paris. **p84** *Two Men Fishing*, c.1880. Drawing: black crayon & scratchwork with gesso, incised, 25.6 x 34.4 cm (10 x 13.5 in). Fogg Art Museum, Harvard University Art Museums (bequest of Meta & Paul J Sachs). **p86** *The Studio Boat*, 1876. Oil, 80 x 100 cm (31.5 x 39.4 in). Collection Galerie Robert Schmit, Paris. **p87** *The Seine at Vétheuil*, 1879–82 Oil, 43.5 x 70.5 cm (17 x 27.75 in). Musée d'Orsay, Paris. **p90** *The Manneporte, Etretat*, 1883. Oil, 65.4 x 81.3 cm (25.75 x 32 in). Metropolitan Museum of Art, New York (bequest of Wm. Church Osborn 1951). **p91** Top: *The Cliff Walk at Pourville*, 1882. Oil, 66.5 x 82.3 cm (26 x 32.4 in). Art Institute of Chicago (Lewis Larned Coburn Memorial Collection 1933). **p91** Right: *Etretat: The Needle and the Porte d'Aval*, 1882–86. Oil on panel, gilded edge, 85.5 x 44 cm (33.67 x 17.3 in). Art Gallery of Ontario. **p92** Hiroshige: Coloured woodblock print of a rocky coast from *Famous Views of Various Provinces* 1853–6. Victoria & Albert Museum, London. **p93** *Cliffs at Etretat*, 1885, from Monet's sketchbook MM 5131. Pencil, 11.5 x 19.5 cm (4.53 x 7.67 in). Musée Marmottan, Paris. **p94** *Cows on a Riverbank*, c.1895–90, from Monet's sketchbook MM 5129. Pencil, 24 x 31.5 cm (9.5 x 12.4 in). Musée Marmottan, Paris. **p95** *The Signal: Gare St Lazare*, 1876. Oil, 65.5 x 81.5 (25.78 x 32 in). Niedersachsisches Landesmuseum, Hanover. **p98** *Bordighera*, 1884. Oil, 64.8 x 81.3 cm (25.5 x 32 in). Metropolitan Museum of Art, New York (bequest of Miss Adelaide Milton de Groot 1967). **p99** *Antibes seen from the Plateau Notre-Dame*, 1888. Oil, 65.7 x 81.3 cm (25.9 x 32 in). Museum of Fine Arts, Boston (Juliana Cheney Edwards Collection). **p100** Hiroshige: Coloured woodblock print from *One Hundred Famous Views in Edo*, c.1857. Victoria and Albert Museum.

CHAPTER 5
p102 *A Branch of the Seine near Giverny*, 1887. Oil, 75 x 92.5 cm (29.5 x 36 in). Musée d'Orsay, Paris. **p103** Theodore Robinson: *Pencil drawing of Claude Monet*, 1910, after a photograph. **p106** *Grainstacks: End of Summer: Morning Effect*, 1891. Oil, 60.5 x 100.5 cm (23.8 x 39.56 in). Musée d'Orsay, Paris. **p107** *Grainstacks, End of Summer: Evening Effect*, 1891. Oil, 60 x 100 cm (23.6 x 39.3 in). Art Institute of Chicago (Arthur M. Wood in memory of Pauline Palmer Wood 1985). **p109** *Grainstacks*, 1888–91, from Monet's sketchbook MM 5134. Pencil, 12 x 18 cm (4.7 x 7.1 in). Musée Marmottan, Paris. **p110** *Poplars in Sunlight*, 1891. Oil, 88 x 93 cm (34.6 x 36.6 in). Aquavella Gallery, New York. **p111** *Poplars Series: Effect of Wind*, 1891. Oil, 100 x 74cm (39.3 x 29in). Document Collection Durand-Ruel, Paris. **p112** Hiroshige: *Nizamu, Yellow Dusk*; woodblock print from the series *53 Stations of the Tokaido*. Museum of Fine Arts, Boston (Bigelow Collection). **p114** *Portail St Romain, Rouen Cathedral: Morning Effect*, 1894. Oil, 100 x 65cm (39.3 x 25.6in). Folkwang Museum, Essen. **p115** *Rouen Cathedral, West Façade: Sunlight*, 1894. Oil, 100.2 x 66 cm (39.4 x 26 in). National Gallery of Art, Washington (Chester Dale Collection). **p119** *Rouen Cathedral, West Façade*, 1894. Oil, 100.4 x 66 cm (39.5 x 26 in). National Gallery of Art, Washington. **p121** Manzana Pissarro: *Monet Painting in the Flowers at Giverny*, 1917. Black pencil, 25 x 21 cm (9.8 x 8.3 in). Private Collection, Mentone. **p123** *House of the Customs Officer, Varengeville*, 1897. Oil, 65.4 x 92.1 cm (25.75 x 36.25 in). Fogg Art Museum, Harvard University Art Museums (Gift of Ella Milbank Foshay). **p127** *London, the Parliament: a Ray of Sunshine Through Fog*, 1904. Oil, 81 x 92 cm (32 x 36.2 in). Musée d'Orsay, Paris.

CHAPTER 6
p130 *The Artist's Garden at Giverny*, 1900. Oil, 81 x 92 cm (32 x 36.2 in). Musée d'Orsay, Paris. **p134** *The Water-lily Pond and the Bridge: Harmony in Green*, 1899. Oil, 89 x 93.5 cm (35 x 36.8 in). Musée d'Orsay, Paris. **p135** *The Rose Arches, Giverny*, 1913. Oil, 81 x 92.5 cm (32 x 36.4 in). Phoenix Art Museum, Arizona (gift of Mr & Mrs Donald D. Harrington). **p137** Hiroshige: *Wisteria*, woodblock print from the series *100 Famous Views in Edo*. Museum of Fine Arts, Boston (Bigelow Collection). **p139** *Palazzo da Mula, Venice*, 1908. Oil, 62 x 81.1 cm (24.4 x 32 in). National Gallery of Art, Washington (Chester Dale Collection). **p143** *The House, Giverny*, c.1922. Oil, 81 x 92 cm (32 x 36.2 in). Musée Marmottan, Paris. **p146–7** *Water Lilies: Study of Water – The Clouds*, 1922–6. Oil, triptych, 197 x 127 cm (77.6 x 50 in). Galérie de l'Orangerie, Paris. **p150** *Self-Portrait*, c.1917. Oil, 70 x 55 cm (27.56 x 21.6 in). Musée d'Orsay, Paris.

$\mathcal{I}$NDEX

Acknowledgements

The publishers would like to thank the following for supplying photographs for this book:
Barnaby's /Ann Meo: 17, 25. Bibliothèque de la Ville de Paris: Photo G. Leyris: 56. Bibliothèque Nationale: 11, 14 (*left*), 20, 23 (*left*), 26, 28 (*right*), 29, 32 (*left*), 34, 37, 41, 48, 52, 60 (*right*), 64, 68, 89, 94 (*below*), 124 (*right*), 125, 148 (*left*). Bridgeman: 38; Bridgeman/Giraudon: 131. Documents from Archives Durand-Ruel: 88 (*left*), 103, 117, 131, 145, 148. Grob/Kharbine/Tapabor: 28. Peter Jackson Collection: 126, 128-129. Mansell Collection: 8, 16, 32 (*right*), 44, 45, 96, 113, 124. Mary Evans Picture Library: 73. Musée Boudin, Honfleur: 14 (*right*). Musée Marmottan, Paris: 80, 132, 136, 138, 140, 144. Philippe Piguet Collection: Back cover, 79, 104, 116, 141, 144. Private Collections: 23 (*right*), 50, 60 (*left*), 62. Reunion des Musées Nationaux, Paris: Front cover, frontispiece, 10, 58, 59, 74, 83, 87, 102, 106, 127, triptych: 146-147, 150. Scala Fotografie: 39. Sirot-Angel Collection, Paris: 24, 28 (*left*), 35 (*right*), 42, 73, 76 (*left*), 93 (*left*), 97. Agence Roger Viollet: 9, 40, 53, 61, 65, 120; Cap/Viollet: 105, 122; Harlingue/Viollet: 133. Jean Vigne, Paris/ Bibliothèque Municipale de Versailles: 88 (*right*), 108.

The publishers would also like to thank the publishers of the following books for permission to reproduce material in this volume: *Claude Monet, biographie et catalogue raisonné*, Daniel Wildenstein, 4 vols., Lausanne-Paris, La Bibliothèque des Arts, 1974-1985; *Les Archives de l'Impressionisme*, vols. 1-4, ed. Lionello Venturi, Editions Durand-Ruel, 1939; *Claude Monet*, Gustave Geffroy, 1922, Les Editions G. Cres. et co.; *Monet: A Retrospective*, Charles Stuckey, Levin Associates, Connecticut, USA, 1985.
All translations are by the author.